Praise for

You Can't Make Me (But I Can Be Persuaded)

"I love the practical strategies and valuable insights from the hearts and lives of strong-willed kids—including Cynthia herself! You'll definitely want to make this book part of your parenting library."

—Dr. Kevin Leman, *New York Times* best-selling
author of *Have a New Kid by Friday*

"In *You Can't Make Me,* Cynthia Tobias provides help and hope for all of us with a strong-willed child of any age. Her extremely practical and time-tested tips will show you how to provide the strong-willed child love balanced with limits, relationship balanced with rules, coaching balanced with cheerleading, and discipleship balanced with discipline. This book will be worth its weight in gold to you and your strong-willed child."

—Walt Larimore, MD, best-selling author
of *God's Design for the Highly Healthy Teen*
and *Why A.D.H.D. Doesn't Mean Disaster*

"Parenting was never designed to be easy, and parenting a strong-willed child can be daunting. Cynthia Tobias has written a book designed to encourage parents to celebrate their children—yes, *even* if they are strong willed! I love how she has provided tried and true strategies that will bring out the best in our children. Her inclusion of stories from parents who are 'in the trenches' serves to remind us that successful parenting is possible for all of us. I love Cynthia's wisdom—but her heart for children made me love this book!"

—JANET PARSHALL, nationally syndicated talk-show host

"At Focus on the Family, we often hear from parents who are frustrated and burned out by their strong-willed kids. Cynthia Tobias's book is tailor-made for them. It will help moms and dads not only address the challenges but also embrace the blessings of having a strong-willed child."

—JIM DALY, president of Focus on the Family

"*You Can't Make Me* is a must-read for every parent of a strong-willed child. Cynthia Tobias is the go-to expert on this subject, and you can't afford to miss out on her incredibly helpful guidance. This book is insightful, grounded, and immeasurably practical. Read it today and start bringing out the best in your strong-willed child!"

—DRS. LES AND LESLIE PARROTT, authors
of *The Parent You Want to Be*

"What a great book! So simple yet so profound. Time and time again I have recommended this book to teachers and parents. Growing up a strong-willed child and having one, I know first-hand how valuable the tools and ideas are in this book. Every parent and teacher should read this!"

—MARY RICE HOPKINS, popular family/children's
recording artist

You Can't
Make Me
[But I Can Be Persuaded]

You Can't Make Me

[But I Can Be Persuaded]

Strategies for Bringing Out the Best in Your
Strong-Willed Child

Cynthia Ulrich Tobias

WATERBROOK
PRESS

You Can't Make Me (But I Can Be Persuaded), Revised and Updated Edition
Published by WaterBrook Press
12265 Oracle Boulevard, Suite 200
Colorado Springs, Colorado 80921

Details in some anecdotes and stories have been changed to protect the identities of the persons involved.

ISBN 978-1-57856-565-8
ISBN 978-0-307-73113-5 (electronic)

Cover design by Mark D. Ford; photography by Tomek Sikora, The Image Bank

Published in the United States by WaterBrook Multnomah, an imprint of the Crown Publishing Group, a division of Random House Inc., New York.

WaterBrook and its deer colophon are registered trademarks of Random House Inc.

Library of Congress Cataloging-in-Publication Data
Tobias, Cynthia Ulrich, 1953–
    You can't make me (but I can be persuaded) : strategies for bringing out the best in your strong-willed child / Cynthia Ulrich Tobias. — Rev. and updated ed.
        p. cm.
    Includes bibliographical references (p.   ).
    ISBN 978-1-57856-565-8 — ISBN 978-0-307-73113-5 (electronic)
  1. Problem children—Behavior modification—United States. 2. Problem children—Family relationships—United States. 3. Problem children—United States—Conduct of life. 4. Child psychology—United States. 5. Individuality in children—United States. 6. Discipline in children—United States. I. Title.
    HQ773.T63 2012
    649'.64—dc23

                                    2012014743

Printed in the United States of America
2014—Revised and Updated Edition

16 15 14 13 12 11 10 9 8 7

To my strong-willed dad,
Robert Ulrich,
who has consistently shown me how to use
my strong-willed nature in a way
that brings honor and glory to God.

◆ ◆ ◆

And to my strong but very patient, compliant mother,
Minnie Ulrich,
who has never quit praying for both of us!

Contents

Contents

Part III: How to Bring Out the Best
in Tough Situations

Contents

Here's How I Know It Works!

My very own strong-willed child, Mike, came bursting through the door with his usual force and energy. He was fresh from yet another week of being a counselor at a summer YMCA camp. I marveled at how quickly the years have passed and here he was—twenty years old and about to enter his junior year in college. Could it possibly be?

"Mom, I have to tell you something."

I've learned to appreciate every opportunity to talk about his life, so I stopped what I was doing and listened.

"The camp kids were driving me crazy. I was so frustrated, I was ready to scream." He paused and put his finger in the air to make a pronouncement. "So, I decided I'd better read one of your books."

I raised my eyebrows. "Which book did you read, Mike?"

He shrugged and grinned. *"You Can't Make Me."* Before I could react he rushed on. "And you know what? *It works!*"

I wasn't prepared for this. Was this my strong-willed child, who appears in every chapter of the book, telling me he was now using it to understand the kids he was counseling at camp?

For the next twenty minutes Mike regaled me with examples he had read in the book, emphasizing the strategies he had used successfully with his campers. We reminisced over stories from the book that he remembered and laughed about the ones he had forgotten or was too young to recall.

Since the first edition of *You Can't Make Me! (But I Can Be Persuaded)* came out in 1999, literally thousands of parents and educators have taken the time to actually write or personally deliver overwhelmingly positive and grateful responses to the powerful and effective strategies in the book. I've been humbled and encouraged to see the hope in their eyes and hear the joy in their voices.

But I have to tell you, by far the most meaningful endorsement I could ask for is the one from Mike. After twenty years of living with and loving my strong-willed child, after the prayers and tears, trial and error, perseverance and frustration, failure and success, he is reading and endorsing the book that describes him as the quintessential strong-willed kid.

So as you read this revised and updated version of *You Can't Make Me,* believe me when I say I'm still in the trenches with you. I've parented a great strong-willed child and his equally wonderful but more compliant twin brother. I will never be able to make the claim I did everything right. Far from it! I am eternally grateful that God has been gracious in supplementing my well-intentioned and often inadequate efforts with His grace, love, and wisdom.

My fervent prayer is that you will benefit from the wisdom and advice of the many strong-willed children and their parents you are about to meet in this book. Most of all, no matter how things turn out, I pray you will be glad you never gave up on the relationship with your strong-willed child. You'll never be able to truly measure the difference it will make.

Part I

Defining the
Strong-Willed Child

Now here's a surprise:
The master praised the crooked manager!
And why? Because he knew how to look
after himself. Streetwise people are smarter
in this regard than law-abiding citizens.
They are on constant alert, looking for angles,
surviving by their wits. I want you to be smart
in the same way—but for what is right—using
every adversity to stimulate you
to creative survival, to concentrate your attention
on the bare essentials, so you'll live, really live,
and not complacently just get by
on good behavior.

—Luke 16:8–9

1

Who Qualifies as a Strong-Willed Child?

How Can You Be Sure It's Not Just Stubbornness?

A grandmother came around the corner and found her grandchild sitting on the floor, leaning against the wall.

"What! Are you in time-out again?" she asked.

"Oh, Grandma, it's no big deal. I pretty much live here."

◆ ◆ ◆

Richard loved football, but he didn't care much for studying. By his junior year in high school, his grades were so poor, there was no assurance he would even be able to graduate with his class. His parents, it seemed, had tried everything—threats, bribes, promises—to no avail. In desperation, Richard's father issued an ultimatum: "Richard, if you don't get those grades up immediately, you can't play football." And this boy who loved football as much as life itself squared his shoulders, faced his dad, and quietly said, "Then forget football." And everyone lost. Richard lost what he cared about most, and his parents lost what they believed was their only leverage.

◆ ◆ ◆

Guests were about to leave and a mother wanted her three-year-old daughter to say good-bye. Strong willed as she was, the child refused. The mother said, "You don't have to say good-bye—just say *something*."

With that the child waltzed into the room, held out her arms in a ballerina pose, and said, "Ta da!" then walked out of the room. She turned to her mother and said, "There, that should hold them for a while."

◆ ◆ ◆

"Angela!" Exasperation was evident in her mother's voice. "Angela, I said get over here *right this minute*!"

Standing in the aisle of the department store, I watched the face of this beautiful five-year-old suddenly darken into an angry scowl. "No!" she cried. "I want to go see the toys *now*!"

Her mother looked exhausted as she grabbed Angela's hand and began to drag her screaming daughter through the store.

As they passed me, the mother rolled her eyes and muttered, "Just another ordinary day."

◆ ◆ ◆

If you are the parent of a strong-willed child (SWC), you've fought hundreds of battles like this with your own child— probably before he turned two years old. You know how frustrating it can be to see your bright, loving, creative offspring instantly turn into a stubborn, immovable force. What did you do to deserve such defiance? How could your wonderful kid turn into such a monster?

Is it disobedience or determination?

You see them everywhere—these strong-willed kids. You may think they're just stubborn, defiant, difficult, and argumentative. But that's not actually the definition of "strong-willed" at all. Those words describe bad behaviors as a result of strong will that's taken a wrong turn. Strong will, in and of itself, is a very positive trait. A strong-willed person is not easily daunted or discouraged, holds firm convictions, and doesn't often accept defeat. A person using strong will in positive ways is fiercely loyal, determined to succeed, and often extraordinarily devoted to accomplishing goals.

So how do you know whether you truly have an inherently strong-willed child (SWC) or a child who is just temporarily defiant? After all, every individual comes into this world with a wonderfully complex and unique set of traits, characteristics, and temperaments. Research has also shown that we are pre-wired with certain tendencies when it comes to taking in and making sense of information. These preferences, or learning styles, determine how we learn, how we decide what's important, and how we communicate with the rest of the world.

It's not really surprising that two parents, who are probably pretty different from each other already, will have children who are an interesting mix of opposite styles. And if you have a strong-willed child, these differences can be magnified. As parents, we often believe our children should do things our way—after all, we are living proof that our way works! But SWCs may have very strong convictions about doing things that make sense to them too.

As parents, we can often overlook the fact that our children have their own views of the world, and we may wear ourselves out trying to change their basic nature as we try to get them to do things that make sense to us. Parents rarely set out to deliberately frustrate their children. And believe it or not, children don't usually try to intentionally annoy their parents. But when two opposing styles meet, something has to give.

A few years ago on a flight to Orlando, I sat next to a frustrated parent. Bob is a former fighter pilot for the United States Air Force. He was serving as an instructor as he prepared to retire early. I learned quickly that he had five kids and that two of them were driving him crazy. We laughed good-naturedly, and I began to tell him some of the principles I cover in my book *The Way They Learn*. As we talked about the different learning styles, he was intrigued.

"This is beginning to make sense," he claimed. He leaned closer and told me why he was so frustrated with two of his beloved children. "How tough can it be," he asked, "to remember to make a check mark in a little box on the chart posted on the refrigerator?" Before I could reply, he continued. "And don't those kids realize you don't brush your teeth before you put on your pajamas? You put on your pajamas first, then you brush your teeth."

I grinned at him. "Bob, how do you eat M&M'S?"

He replied without hesitation. "Oh, I always eat the primary colors first." He looked puzzled. "Why? How do you eat them?"

"Well, I just sort of pour them in my hand and pop them into my mouth."

"Oh no! Don't you realize that the Mars candy company has no specific formula for how many of each color go into each individual bag? You can't just consume them randomly before you know what you've got!"

I laughed. In jest I said, "Bob, you are a sick man!"

He joined my laughter but suddenly looked thoughtful. "You know, I always thought my children were being disobedient if they didn't do everything my way. I've already figured out what works best and what methods are most efficient. I assumed that if they do it any other way, it's just pure and simple insubordination!"

Bob and I spent the next couple of hours discovering and celebrating the differences between him and his wife and each of their children. He was delighted to read through the learning styles charts and checklists, and he seemed relieved to learn some ways to motivate and inspire his own SWCs.

How strong willed are you or your child?

Strong will, of course, comes in all styles. In over twenty-five years of teaching and working with learning styles full time, however, I have found that SWCs, whether children or adults, have several characteristics in common. Take a few minutes to read the following checklist and mark all the items that describe you personally. Then go through the list again for each of your children and measure the degree of strong will each child appears to possess.

Checking your SWC quotient

Mark only those statements that are true *most* of the time for each member of the family:

The Strong-Willed Child (SWC)...

almost never accepts words like "impossible" or phrases like "it can't be done."

Parent 1 _____ Parent 2 _____ Child 1 _____ Child 2 _____

can move with lightning speed from being a warm, loving presence to being a cold, immovable force.

Parent 1 _____ Parent 2 _____ Child 1 _____ Child 2 _____

may argue the point into the ground, sometimes just to see how far into the ground the point will go.

Parent 1 _____ Parent 2 _____ Child 1 _____ Child 2 _____

if bored, has been accused of actually creating a crisis rather than have a day go by without incident.

Parent 1 _____ Parent 2 _____ Child 1 _____ Child 2 _____

considers rules to be more like guidelines ("As long as I'm abiding by the 'spirit of the law,' why are you being so picky?").

Parent 1 _____ Parent 2 _____ Child 1 _____ Child 2 _____

shows great creativity and resourcefulness—seems to always find a way to accomplish a goal.

Parent 1 _____ Parent 2 _____ Child 1 _____ Child 2 _____

can turn what seems to be the smallest issue into a grand crusade or a raging controversy.

Parent 1 _____ Parent 2 _____ Child 1 _____ Child 2 _____

doesn't usually do things just because "you're supposed to"—it needs to matter personally.

Parent 1 _____ Parent 2 _____ Child 1 _____ Child 2 _____

often refuses to obey unconditionally—usually wants to negotiate a few terms before complying.

Parent 1 _____ Parent 2 _____ Child 1 _____ Child 2 _____

is not afraid to try the unknown—to conquer the unfamiliar (although each SWC chooses his own risks, they all seem to possess the confidence to try new things).

Parent 1 _____ Parent 2 _____ Child 1 _____ Child 2 _____

can take what was meant to be the simplest request and interpret it as an offensive ultimatum.

Parent 1 _____ Parent 2 _____ Child 1 _____ Child 2 _____

may not actually say the exact words to apologize, but almost always makes things right.

Parent 1 _____ Parent 2 _____ Child 1 _____ Child 2 _____

Your score: How much strong will do you have?

0–3   You've got it, but you don't use it much.

4–7   You use it when you need to, but not on a daily basis.

8–10   You've got a very healthy dose of it, but you can back off when you want to.

11–12 You don't leave home without it—and it's almost impossible not to use it.

It takes one to know one!

I've talked to thousands of SWCs over the past several years, including hundreds of prodigal sons and daughters, and they have given me a wealth of information to share with you. Their answers are consistent, and their insights are valuable.

I've also lived my life seeing firsthand how the mind of the SWC works—from the inside out. I was never what you would call a rebellious or defiant child. I grew up the daughter of a conservative, evangelical preacher, and I never rebelled against my dad or caused him to feel ashamed of me. I was not a particularly loud or obnoxious child. I didn't talk back to teachers. In fact, you couldn't have traced half the trouble I caused back to me! Outwardly, I was quiet and compliant and basically easy to get along with.

But whenever I'm backed into a corner and told, "Do it... or else," I simply choose "else." I may not be confrontational or loud, but I know there is nothing I really *have* to do—except die, which I'm willing to do. And since I'm willing to die and you're not, I win. (Okay, I'm dead, but I win.) As you can imagine, this mind-set has always presented a unique challenge to my parents and others in authority over me. My mother tells me that as early as eighteen months I had already figured out no one could really *make* me do anything. She tried to insist I eat all the food that was placed before me. As soon as I figured out she was going to have me sit there until the food was gone, I simply dumped the remaining contents of the bowl on top of my head. It became a contest each meal to see if Mom could figure out which bite was my last one before the bowl was dumped and she had a mess to clean up. It didn't take long for her to decide the battle wasn't worth it!

My sister came along five years after I did, and she was nothing like me. Since it probably took my parents that long to work up the courage to have another child, I think they were relieved to find that Sandee was compliant and pleasant natured. As the oldest, I used my position and strong-willed nature to both delight and traumatize my sister. I was definitely in charge, and Sandee followed my lead. Sometimes perceived as the bully or the dictator as well as the role model and encourager, I enjoyed having my sister recognize and appreciate my strengths.

Although my mother was convinced that even as adults we would never be able to do anything but fight with each other, Sandee and I are very close and enjoy a wonderful relationship. People often ask her if she grew up resenting me because I was such an SWC. She sweetly smiles and claims it was actually a blessing. "You see," she explains, "I loved it. Since Cindy was always the one with the dangerous or adventurous ideas, I was never the one to get in trouble. I would just say it wasn't my idea, wasn't my fault—and Mom knew I was telling the truth."

Even though I'm an SWC, I believe my best credential for speaking out on behalf of all SWCs is that I'm the parent of a strong-willed son. (My mother denies she prayed this would happen so I would know what it was like!) My son Mike was a typical SWC. One moment he was loving and thoughtful, the next he was relentlessly terrorizing his brother or mouthing off to his dad.

I've been forced to live what I teach every day. I'm not giving you advice from a quiet corner. I know firsthand that having an SWC can seem like both the best and the worst thing that can happen to you. My SWC, Mike, is strong and intelligent and determined. He can ruthlessly drive himself to master a task or achieve a goal. And yet, the strength of his will puts him at risk for bad behavior when obstacles stand in the way of his plans or when someone like his twin brother, Robert, is not his normally compliant self. Mike can quickly change from a focused analytic to a frustrated, impatient person, loudly demanding his way. At times like this, I used to hear him screaming at his brother, "You're *fired,* Robert! You're not my brother anymore!" Of course, if Robert called his bluff and walked away, Mike was quick to call him back, immediately suggesting at least a slight compromise.

An opportunity with great potential

If any of this sounds familiar, you've come to the right place! I'm about to offer you more hope and encouragement about your relationship with your SWC than you may have thought possible. I realize we SWCs can drive you crazy. We know how to push the buttons that can reduce you to rage in a matter of seconds. We seem constantly to choose to do things the hard way. School and other traditional functions may leave us bored, frustrated, and restless.

But if you're the parent of one of these wild and wonderful children, you've been given the opportunity to love, nurture, and guide an individual who has great potential. Although you may have been led to believe that strong will simply denotes defiance, aggressiveness, and rebellion, steely determination does not have to be a negative trait! When you know how to bring out the best in your fiercely independent gift from God, you'll find incredible strength and possibilities in both of you without sacrificing any bottom-line accountability.

Many parents automatically assume that having a strong-willed child is a bad thing. While it can be challenging, by the time you finish reading this book, the chances are very good you will actually be excited you have such a child. It is a great gift to have a child with firm convictions, a high spirit, and a sense of adventure. Why not direct that wonderful and mysterious energy into the right channels, and use that marvelous determination to achieve positive results?

I often remind parents of SWCs that their children may change the world—after all, it's not likely that the world is going to change them! I also tell them that whatever seems to irritate them most about their SWC now is almost certain to be one of their SWC's greatest strengths and keys to success as an adult. You no doubt have a budding young artist, attorney, preacher, salesman, or other future persuasive professional right there in your home—exercising her powers of influence on you. After all, who else can she practice on? Who else do you really *want* her to practice on? Your SWC may be God's instrument for making the world a better place. Think about some of the great leaders and innovators in our past: Thomas Jefferson, Marie Curie, Albert Einstein, Joan of Arc, Thomas Edison, and others. Each of these people held up under adversity, stood up for his or her convictions, and persisted against all odds. They refused to believe their dreams were impossible.

Of course, SWCs often travel a rocky road on the way to their success, and parents will certainly have an abundance of opportunities to develop patience and creative discipline techniques. You will be stretched and challenged beyond what you thought were your limits. But ultimately you can be rewarded with an SWC who loves God, who loves you, and who leaves your home with the ability to be a successful adult.

This book can place in your hands a priceless treasure—the gift of understanding your strong-willed child. I'll give you a glimpse into the mind of an SWC so you can begin to see how it works. I'll offer you practical strategies for how to motivate and inspire your SWC rather than simply to engage in power struggles and pointless battles. I'll give you guidelines to help you determine whether you need to do something drastic. What you are about to read and think about can—if you choose to act on it—heal your relationship with your SWC, bring peace to an argumentative family, and help you discover some wonderful things about yourself in the process.

Most of all, I hope this book shows you that instead of becoming exasperated and irritated with the SWCs in your life, you can honor and value what they do best while still holding them accountable for moral and spiritual values.

Real wisdom, God's wisdom, begins
with a holy life and is characterized
by getting along with others.... You can develop
a healthy, robust community that lives right
with God and enjoy its results only if you do
the hard work of getting along with each other,
treating each other with dignity and honor.

—James 3:17–18

2

How Is the Strong-Willed Child Wired?

Do You Know What We're Thinking?

I've been writing and teaching about the strong-willed child for more than twenty-five years. During that time I've talked to hundreds and hundreds of strong-willed people of all ages on six continents, in all walks of life, Christian and non-Christian, criminals and law-abiding citizens, tattooed and not. What you are about to read is a consensus among this diverse population of strong-willed individuals (including me) who agree on some basic fundamental truths about how strong-willed minds are wired.

Three crucial truths about how we think

1. It's not authority we have trouble with; it's how the authority is communicated.

Even some of the most openly rebellious strong-willed kids insist they don't have trouble with authority. We SWCs wouldn't respect our parents if they drew the line and moved it. We wouldn't respect the government if there were laws, but no one enforced them. It's not the issue of authority; it's how the authority is *communicated*. What sets us off is your finger in our face as you tell us to "do it or else." SWCs know you're not really the "big boss"; we always have a choice whether to obey or take the consequences. If you use your authority in a way that suggests we don't have a choice, there's almost always going to be trouble. We usually don't respond well when you simply issue orders to be obeyed. We want to be treated with respect, and we respond best to a voice that's calm and firm. If your authority is transmitted to us by shouting or with angry words and gestures, we tend to simply tune you out—and prepare for battle.

When I was growing up, my dad was the ultimate authority in our house. My SWC nature did not question him when he laid down the law. But you see, Dad intuitively knew a parenting technique that is critical for dealing with the SWC. If he said, "Stop *now*!" I just stopped. I didn't question or argue. I knew my dad wouldn't talk to me like that unless it was essential that I obeyed. And that could save my life if it stopped me from stepping in front of a speeding car. If he had talked to me with the same urgency and firmness all the time, I would have tuned him out and probably not done much of anything he asked.

Here's the point: If you use the same angry tone of voice for everything—"You get upstairs to bed!" "You eat the rest of that dinner!" "You get dressed right now!"—you'll find your SWC *arguing* with you about everything.

Some parents think it will signal weakness if they speak politely to a child instead of bluntly "laying down the law." The fact is, you may be amazed at how much easier it is to get strong-willed children to cooperate when, instead of angrily shouting, "Get downstairs right now and get in that car!" you calmly say, "The car leaves in two minutes—let's go!"

2. Strong-willed children don't need to control you; they just can't let you take all control away from them.

Remember, we know we always have a choice. That means we have ultimate control over what we will and will not do. When SWCs are told, "You will…" or "You're going to…" or "This is how it's going to be…," we may interpret that kind of speech as an attempt to take all control away from us, and we can't let you do that. SWCs need to keep at least *some* control over our own lives. So when we feel cornered, we may end up exercising the only option we have left—even if it's unpleasant or harmful. In the following chapters, you'll discover some very effective strategies for sharing control with your SWC without compromising your authority, a concept I found invaluable in my own parenting.

One cold winter morning when my son Mike was only

four, he started to walk out the door without his sweater. Because I know how an SWC's mind works, I offered him an option. "Mike, do you want to wear your red sweater or your blue sweater?"

Quick as a flash, he turned to me and replied, "I don't want to wear a sweater."

I had to fight my natural response, which was to tell him he certainly *was* going to wear a sweater and he had better decide which one or I was going to decide for him. But I knew I couldn't *make* him wear anything. Would this battle be worth ruining our morning together? Swallowing my frustration, I asked him another question. "Mike, what do you want to wear to keep warm?"

He paused for a moment and shrugged before he stated in a matter-of-fact manner, "I want to wear Daddy's sweater."

Again I fought my desire to tell him that was totally absurd and to put on his own sweater. I asked Daddy if Mike could wear one of his sweaters, and he agreed. My four-year-old SWC was almost lost inside it. He looked ridiculous, and I wanted to attach a sign to his back that read, "My mother didn't dress me!" Instead, I tucked one of Mike's sweaters under my arm and we went on with our day.

It took less than fifteen minutes for Mike to grow weary of struggling with the oversized sweater. Resisting the urge to say, "I told you so," I casually asked if he would like to have his own sweater instead of Daddy's. Without hesitating, he nodded, took off the bulky garment and put on his own. Just like that. No big deal.

You can and should enforce the rules, but the reality is that you cannot *force* SWCs to *comply* with the rules. Be careful about backing yourself into a corner by telling SWCs what they will and will not do. What if they decide to prove you wrong?

3. The quality of the relationship we have determines the effectiveness of your parenting strategies.

In the heat of the battle, parents often forget the most critical component of effective parenting: if you have the kind of relationship with your child that she wants to preserve, you have some valuable leverage. If SWCs really enjoy spending time with you when we're *not* in trouble, we'll do our best to stay on your good side. On the other hand, what do we have to gain by obeying if you're always yelling at us anyway? What's the up side? One bonus here is that you don't have to be the best parent in the neighborhood; you don't have to be the most creative, energetic, or intelligent adult in your child's life. The other bonus? If you work at keeping a healthy relationship, your child will have the best reason in the world to obey you and follow your guidance.

When it comes to building and maintaining a quality relationship, here are three key elements to remember:

- *Relationships will always matter more than rules.* If we have a good relationship with you, we'll follow your rules even if we don't agree with them. We do it because we love and respect *you.*
- *Home should be a place we always look forward to coming back to*—a safe harbor where we are understood and valued for who we are. We know you want to prepare us for dealing with a hostile world, but if you don't provide a safe, warm place for us, who will?
- *We need to know that you'll always be there for us, no matter what.* That doesn't mean you should let the SWC take advantage of you. It means your love for us is unshakable and unconditional. That same love must sometimes be tough, and it doesn't just bail us out when we get in trouble. Above all, no matter what we say or do, no matter what consequences must be faced, we have to know your love will never disappear.

What the SWC really wants

Although you'll always be challenged by your SWC, it may be reassuring to know there are some fairly predictable issues that will come up at certain ages or stages.

The toddler years

What the SWC Is Thinking: I seek to control whatever part of myself or my environment that I can. I learn at a very early age they can't *make* me digest peas. They can pry my little mouth open and put the peas in and I may accidentally swallow a couple, but I alone will decide whether they stay down or come back up. It's an amazing discovery for a strong-willed toddler! My parents may be ten times stronger or older or smarter, but there are certain things they just can't *make* me do! It doesn't take me long to figure out where I can exercise control over what I do and do not *have* to do. Potty training? No matter how important it is to my mom, I still have the last word. Time-out? Well, you may have to stand on the other side of the door the whole time to keep me in the room. Wear the clothes you put on me? You can't hold me every second, and when you let me go I can take those clothes off in the blink of an eye.

How to Shape Your Response: From the very beginning, your strong-willed offspring will be testing what the boundaries are and how much of their universe they can control. If you're a strong-willed person yourself, you know better than anyone why this is happening, but it's sure not the same when you're the *parent* instead of the child!

Figure out as early as possible how you can voluntarily give your child some control over herself, even in very small ways. Don't just give her the toy you want her to have—let her have a choice. If she's determined to walk up those stairs without you, stay close enough to ensure her safety, but let her take the time she needs to struggle up one step at a time. If she wants to carry that dirty ragged blanket into church, swallow your pride and let her have it. Save the conflict for the very important battles you will need to fight later.

Remember to celebrate the ways your SWC is already learning to think and act independently—you have a front-row seat to watch your child develop into an amazing individual!

The elementary years

What the SWC Is Thinking: I'm trying to figure out why I have to do something just because you said so. Why do I have to keep my room clean? Why do I have to do that stupid homework? Why do I have to go to school when I don't learn anything anyway? Why doesn't anyone want to answer my questions?

How to Shape Your Response: Whoa, you thought it might get easier as they got older! Childhood is an adventure for your strong-willed child, and you may often find yourself running to keep up. I know—you're the parent and you know best, but that independent, stubborn son or daughter just doesn't want to take your word for it. Unfortunately, these are usually the busiest years, with working parents and soccer games and baseball practices and choir performances and teacher conferences. It would make life so much easier if your children would just do what you said without the endless arguments and questions! But you know that's not how the strong-willed mind works. If we want to know something, we'll keep up a dogged pursuit of answers until we practically drive you crazy. How will you cope?

Here's where it's especially important to remember a critical question: *What's the point?* Instead of going into endless detail, just cut to the chase—give your child the bottom line. Remember, you want bottom-line accountability, and that means your SWC doesn't call the shots on the end result; the compromise can come by allowing some flexibility in the *method,* not the outcome.

"Look, here's the deal. The bottom line is that your homework has to be done by eight tomorrow morning. If you want to wake up an hour early to do it, that's fine. If you want to do it in ten minute spurts, that's fine, too—as long as when we leave for school at eight in the morning, we take the finished homework with us."

"You don't want to do the dishes? Fine. But everyone has a chore to do. Maybe you can get your sister to trade with you tonight."

Don't engage in arguments over methods—focus on the outcomes. Try writing this question on a piece of paper and taping it to your refrigerator:

What's the point?

This approach won't stop all the questions, but it sure will go a long way toward shorter answers.

The teenage years

What the SWC Is Thinking: Leave me alone—but don't go away! All I ever hear is, "You're not wearing *that,* are you?" "You better watch your mouth." "You'll never get to college with these grades!" What I want to know is, when are they going to trust me? When will my parents start treating me like a grownup? Sometimes I think they don't even like me anymore.

How to Shape Your Response: Something about adolescence makes kids believe everyone is constantly bugging them about everything. They're trying to establish their independence and individuality, but it seems like all the authority figures are just trying to keep a thumb on them. It's not that teen SWCs want to be completely free of family—after all, there are lots of perks to living at home. They enjoy the laundry service, the good meals, and the financial underwriting of many projects. But they wonder why they can't have things *their* way sometimes.

Not every strong-willed teenager is destined to become rebellious or difficult to live with, but when a wild streak sets in, even the most dedicated parent can face some daunting challenges. As you know, there aren't many simple answers, but here are a couple of tried-and-true guidelines that can really help keep peace and harmony in the family:

1. Guide—don't dictate.

Every teenager needs to know how to motivate himself before he leaves home. Instead of telling your teenager what to do and how to do it, try deciding together what needs to be accomplished and ask your SWC what it will take to motivate him. He needs to be thinking about what it will take to get himself to do something he doesn't want to do instead of having a parent automatically step in and give unsolicited advice and suggestions.

We SWCs want to know what the purpose of a goal or task is, mostly so we can decide whether it's worth the effort to achieve it. After all, who established the goal in the first place? Why? Once we understand what the end result is supposed to be, what if we can find a better way to get there? SWCs are not usually trying to irritate you by posing these questions. Instead, we're genuinely attempting to figure out what to think and how to stay in control of our world.

You're needed more now as a guide and resource than as a supervisor and taskmaster. There will still be issues you'll go to the wall for—physical safety, moral values, etc.—but choosing your battles is more important now than ever.

2. We do better with compelling problems to solve than with a list of chores to do.

Instead of just handing down the to-do lists and issuing the rules and regulations, try soliciting input from a very creative and often untapped source—your strong-willed teenager. Put forth the compelling problem you need to have solved, and be sincere and open-minded when you ask for input. You already know what you want to have done, but what if there's another way to accomplish the same goal? Share the problem, and you may be surprised at how quickly and willingly your teen can help you get the job done.

My sister found that her SWC, Tracy, consistently resisted taking the trash out to the curb on Monday nights. No amount of reminders or punishment for forgetting was effective. Finally, Sandee talked to Tracy after dinner one night. "Tracy, we have to figure out how to make sure the trash gets taken out on Monday nights. I get home from work too late to do it, and your sisters don't even think about it. Can you help me figure out a way to get it done?" Within two days Tracy had a chart on the refrigerator with reminders for both her sisters and herself and weekly assignments for who would be responsible for taking out the trash. They never missed another trash day—and Tracy took great pride in tackling a problem no one else seemed able to solve.

When young adult SWCs move back home

I remember reading a poster years ago that said, "Children who leave home to set the world on fire often come back for more matches." You think if you get them all the way through school they'll be on their own, but somehow they show up on your doorstep looking for a way back into your safe harbor. In many ways it's a compliment that you're the one they want to come back to, but it doesn't take long to discover there's a whole new set of issues when your SWC is no longer your minor child. You don't have the same leverage you did when they were under eighteen, but whether your SWC is six or twenty-six, you can still use the sound principles you're reading in this book.

What happens when your adult SWC turns into an unmotivated, discouraged houseguest who missed getting the dream job and has lost all interest in fighting the uphill battle of finding a place in this world? What was true when they were children is still true now. You can't let them get by with bad behavior. You should hold them accountable for outcomes and continually shift responsibility to them for their actions and results.

It's more important than ever to include your SWC in the problem-solving process, with questions like these:

- "What do you think is a fair exchange for your living with us?"
- "How will we know we can count on you to stay accountable?"
- "How would you prefer we approach you if we feel you might be taking advantage of us?"
- "How can we help you achieve the goals you're setting for yourself?"
- "What's the best way for us to show we love you?"

In the following chapters you'll find a wealth of information that will work regardless of the age of your SWC. None of it expires when they grow up, and it's never too late to use these tried-and-true strategies. If you hold steady and stick to what works, they won't stay home forever!

A reminder for parenting all ages

Your strong-willed child will always keep you challenged. You won't have to worry about becoming bored or getting into a rut. There's something to be said for that!

But life is too short to constantly battle with those you love. If you can begin to understand the inner workings of an SWC's mind, you may hold the key to her heart.

It sure beats knocking down the door!

Part II

How to Bring Out the Best in a Strong-Willed Child

God can do anything, you know—far more

than you could ever imagine or guess

or request in your wildest dreams!

He does it not by pushing us around

but by working within us,

his Spirit deeply and gently within us.

—Ephesians 3:20

3

How Can I Turn Conflict into Cooperation?

Five Proven Strategies to Help You Both Thrive

As mentioned earlier, I grew up as a preacher's kid. I never rebelled against my dad—in fact, we have such a strong relationship that even now, as a grown woman with kids of my own, I wouldn't dream of doing something that disappoints him. I didn't talk back to teachers; I wasn't loud, rebellious, or rude. Outwardly, I've always been relatively cooperative. But again, if you point your bony finger in my face and say, "Do it or else!"— I'll choose "else." I know there's nothing I really *have* to do except die—which I'm willing to do (at least figuratively).

If you're reading this book, I'm pretty sure you know what I'm talking about. Standard methods of discipline and motivation often just don't work with an SWC who knows you can't really *make* him do anything and who isn't concerned about the consequences if he doesn't obey. So what can you do? How do you hold on to your parental authority without losing either your relationship or your mind?

Remember, I've talked to hundreds of SWCs of all ages and stages in life, and what you're reading reflects a strong consensus among all of us. What I'm about to share with you is the list of the top five strategies SWCs have agreed will succeed more often than they fail. These strategies work for all kids, but they are absolutely *critical* for the SWC. They probably won't sound new to you—but you will be surprised and relieved to find out that the way you use them can make a world of difference in how your SWCs respond to you.

If it sounds too good to be true, find a trusted friend or family member who is also an SWC and ask if that individual would mind reading this section and telling you if it's really true. Two things will almost certainly happen: First, your SWC friend or family member will assure you that you are *not* having difficulty because you are a failure as a parent; and second, they'll confirm that you can anticipate measurable improvements in your relationship with your SWC by simply understanding how to communicate what you need and expect without engaging in battle. I also recommend staying in touch with your SWC friend or family member and asking them for a little advice and feedback when you need it. You can say something like, "I have a kid who's a lot like you. I wonder if you could give me an idea of what might work."

So here they are—Five to Thrive tips for bringing out the best in a strong-willed child. If you try these with an open mind and loving heart, you'll be amazed at the results.

1. Choose your battles. Don't make everything nonnegotiable.

If you make a big deal out of everything, pretty soon everything will be a big deal, and you may get to the point where you'll hear some absolutely ridiculous arguments designed purely to get a reaction out of you:

"It's a cat."

"No, it's not. It's a dog."

"I'm your mom."

"No, you're not. You're my dad."

And so on.

We know you can't be the boss of everything, so we may decide to prove you're not the boss of anything. Decide which issues are actually worth going to the wall for—and go to the wall for them. Issues of moral and spiritual values and those of physical safety are certainly big deals. You're not going to let your children ride without a seat belt or walk into traffic. You're not going to let them lie or cheat or steal or hurt anyone. But if you can relinquish some control over smaller issues like precisely what they wear or how they say something or their method of emptying a trash can, you'll find your SWC cooperating with you much better than if she has to do every little thing *exactly* your way.

My SWC, Mike, was at the breakfast table with his brother, Rob, when they were about eight years old. "Hey, Rob," Mike said. "Pass me that cereal."

I looked at him in surprise. "Mike! What do you say?"

Without skipping a beat, he said, "Rob, pass me that cereal. Do it now."

I shook my head. "Michael Tobias, you know better than—"

"I'm not going to say that word," he quickly declared, "and you can't make me. If you make me say that word, I won't eat breakfast."

I nodded my head. "That's fine, because this one's worth it, Michael Tobias. I won't raise a rude, ill-mannered child—this one's *worth* it."

He got up, stomped down the hall to his room, and slammed the door. Less than a minute later he stomped back down the hall, sat down at the table, and said loudly through gritted teeth, "*Please.*"

You know what I wanted to say, right? I wanted to tell him that's not how we say it and start over from the beginning. But

I did then what I had to do at least once or twice a week: I covered my mouth with my hand and said nothing. I had just won my go-to-the-wall issue. If I kept picking at him to do it a certain way, I'd lose everything.

When I speak to groups of young moms, one area of conflict comes up over and over. "She always wants to dress herself in the morning, and she chooses clothes that don't match!" "He wants to wear the most ridiculous things!" The conflict usually turns into a really big deal and everyone leaves the house frustrated and angry. My advice is almost always the same: Why not try filling the drawers only with clothes that match? Or you could buy a lanyard with a tag that says, "I dressed myself today"!

There won't be any shortage of conflicts as you deal with your SWC, but you can greatly reduce the number of battles by just remembering one thing: ask yourself if it's really worth it. Is this a go-to-the-wall issue? In the grander scheme of things, will it matter a year from now?

2. Lighten up, but don't let up.

I'm sure I don't have to tell you that your SWC will always be just a step ahead of you. "You said don't jump off *that* chair."

Masters of finding and using the loopholes, SWCs take

great satisfaction in proving that you obviously did *not* think of everything. We'll push your buttons and reduce you to rage in a matter of seconds. We know how to make you cry, yell, or throw your hands up in despair. It's a little disconcerting as a child to have this much power, but using it is often irresistible. I push and you react. I push and you react again. I say to myself, "I really shouldn't…," and then I push and you react.

How can you break this habit? Punishment often doesn't work. When you yell, it only confirms our power over you. But one thing has the potential to turn conflict into cooperation more often than you ever thought possible: a sense of humor. Lighten up, but don't let up. You should not let an SWC get by with bad behavior; however, humor will often catch your SWC off guard and may disarm him before he even realizes what's happening. Best of all, it can offer what I call a "fire escape"— an opportunity to pull back gracefully and cooperate.

My favorite way to lighten up is to use this two-word phrase: *Nice try.* The next time your SWC says or does something that really ticks you off, instead of jumping down his throat, simply say, "Nice try." Then smile and stop talking. Or, "Nice try. I thought you were serious for a minute." Then smile and stop talking. One of two things will happen—either your SWC will back down or he'll dig in his heels and refuse to change. But you just gave him the opportunity to decide, and to save face. Instead of going on the attack, which serves only to reinforce his resistance, you've taken down the first line of defense with the simple tactic of humor. Sometimes you'll still have to do things the hard way, but you'll be surprised at the number of times this works.

My friend Sharon is a strong-willed woman. A no-nonsense mom who doesn't put up with disrespect or disobedience, she also knows how to bring out the best in her SWC. Brandon was sixteen when Sharon picked him up from school one day. As he tossed his backpack into the backseat, Sharon asked, "So how was your day, Brandon?"

He was fresh off an animated conversation with his friends. Without even thinking, he answered. "It was *great*, chick."

Dead silence.

Brandon froze in fear, realizing what he had just said. Sharon already had her hand over her mouth to keep from showing her first reaction. She took a deep breath, looked at him, and replied, "That's *Mrs.* Chick to you."

Brandon immediately lowered his head. "Oh, Mom, I'm so sorry!"

Now if he hadn't reacted that way, his mom would have had to do things the hard way and enforce the rule about disrespect. But she gave him a chance to make things right instead of letting anger get the best of her.

It doesn't always work—but wouldn't it be worth trying even if it only worked once in a while? If you practice this, you'll be pleasantly surprised at the number of times humor is effective in disarming a conflict.

3. Ask more questions; issue fewer orders.

If you want an SWC to do something, asking a question that assumes the best in us almost always results in us moving toward what you want us to do. For example, Mike promised to finish his homework before five o'clock so the dining room table could be cleared for dinner. At five, he was still not finished. Instead of saying, "Mike, you said you'd be done by five—get this stuff off the table!" I found that asking a question worked better: "Mike, are you almost done with that homework?"

He jumped and replied, "Oh yeah, just one more problem and I'll get this stuff off the table."

It takes a little practice, but I think you'll be amazed by how effective asking questions can be.

"Robert, have you taken the trash out yet?"

"Oh, I forgot, I'll go do that right now."

"Marie, did you put your homework in your backpack?"

"Oops—I'm on my way to do it right now."

This approach creates a much more positive and cooperative atmosphere than issuing orders: "Robert, you still haven't taken the trash out—get moving!" "Marie, that homework had better be in your backpack!"

One dad came back to me a few days after an SWC seminar and told me, "It doesn't work. That question thing—it doesn't work with my son."

I was surprised. "Are you sure?" I asked. "You're the only one who has ever told me it doesn't work, and I've been telling parents this for years."

Shaking his head vigorously, he said, "No. I'm telling you it just doesn't work."

I thought for a minute, then asked him, "Can you give me an example of the kinds of questions you're asking your son?"

The dad nodded and said, "Sure. Just yesterday I asked him, 'Don't you think it's time to straighten up your attitude?'"

Whoa—no wonder! This dad had just unwittingly used the type of question that almost instantly creates a defensive and angry response. Now I've started including in my seminars some specific types of questions that can actually lower the level of conflict, along with some questions you'll want to avoid using as much as possible.

Questions that can destroy relationships

Here are some key questions that almost always trigger the defenses of an SWC and can destroy relationships:

- Why did you do that?
- When are you going to learn?
- Why can't you just do what you're told?
- What were you thinking?
- What's the matter with you?

If you can't remember these exact questions, just remember this shortcut: never use the words *why* and *you* in the same sentence. For example: "I don't know why you can't just…" or "Why won't you listen?" or "You can't even tell me why…" The combination of those two words in a sentence—*why* and *you*—can be more explosive than you ever intended, since they almost always result in defensiveness and resistance. And once you've engaged in this kind of conflict with your SWC, you're unlikely to achieve a happy ending to the argument.

Questions that can build relationships

The good news is that there are many other questions that can actually build and strengthen relationships as well as reduce conflict. Try using these instead.

Do you want help with that?

I learned when my SWC was just a toddler that I couldn't assume he wanted my help just because he complained about something. "I can't tie my shoe!" didn't mean I should reach over there and do it for him. I needed to ask first, "Would you like me to tie it for you?" Sometimes his answer was yes, sometimes no, but at least he had some say in how much control he was giving away. Later when it came to homework, I would occasionally hear him say, "I hate this homework! I don't understand any of it!" Again, I learned it would not be a good move to simply sit down and begin to go over the assignment with him. I needed to ask, "Would you like some help with that?"

By doing this, I signaled respect for him—and an understanding that he still had control over himself and what he did. By asking before I helped, I was also getting his cooperation right up front, and now whatever we did together would also be his idea.

Are you annoying me on purpose?
This one really took my SWC off guard. "Mike, are you annoying me on purpose?"

He looked surprised, then sheepish. "Yeah, I guess I kinda am."

I smiled. "Well, it's working—knock it off." Then he was smiling, too.

You can use lots of variations on this.

"Are you *trying* to get in trouble?"

"No, is that what I'm doing?"

"Oh, yeah."

This is a great accompaniment to use with your sense of humor strategy.

Do you know why I asked for that?

Most SWCs will tell you they don't have to agree with your reasons for doing something—they just want you to *have* some. It almost never works to keep repeating: *Because I said so.* We're automatically suspicious when you don't want to give us any information. Why do you need unquestioned obedience? How do we know we aren't being asked to do something that goes against our own convictions of what's right or wrong?

We usually don't need you to go into any deep explanations of process or a discussion of philosophy or logic. We just want to know one thing: What's the big deal? When you say, "Do you know why I asked for that?" you create a dialogue in which mutual respect can flourish.

Is that what you meant to do?

Another "fire escape" you can give your SWC is to say something like, "You really hurt your sister's feelings—is that what you meant to do?"

"No."

"I didn't think so. How do you want to make that right?"

See what you're doing as a parent? You're giving the SWC a

chance to explain himself, and you're expecting the best of him. You're also shifting ownership and responsibility for actions back to the SWC. If he says yes, that's what he meant to do, it's a whole different matter. You'll have to do things the hard way and use an effective disciplinary approach, since you can't allow bad behavior to go unchallenged.

Is that what you wanted?

I think this is my favorite question of all. Again, it shifts the responsibility to the SWC and, even more importantly, it gives you as a parent a lot of leverage. For example, let's say your SWC brings home a report card full of Ds and Fs. Your first response may be, "These grades have to come up!" No, they don't. They don't *have* to come up. In the comics, Charlie Brown is famous for saying, "There's no heavier burden than a great potential." And SWCs are familiar with hearing their parents say things like, "You could do so much better than this! You're just not trying hard enough!" That's you telling them what you want and what they should want. But you're not expressing interest in even finding out what your SWC wants and, since we know we always have a choice, we'll almost always resist letting you choose for us.

Try this instead when you're looking at that disappointing report card:

"An F in history. Did you want an F in history?"

"Yes, I did." It's a response designed to get you to react. That SWC knows you can't *make* her want a better grade. So just move on and come back to this grade later.

"An F in English. Did you want an F in English?"

"No."

"What grade did you want?"

"I don't know—at least a C, I guess."

"What do you think it will take to get it?"

"A miracle."

"Do you want any help with that miracle?"

See what you're doing? You're getting the SWC to commit herself to doing better without you demanding she do so. You can tell her all day long how she should change her ways, but until you get her to actually say, "I want a better grade," or, "I don't like living my life this way," you don't have any leverage. It's just the same old thing—everyone telling her what to do. She has to want it for herself before she'll be motivated to make a change.

Say the magic word.

Learning to use these questions requires practice, but with time you'll find it works almost like magic to improve the cooperation level between you and your SWC. Your child will begin to see you as an ally rather than an adversary. And he will almost certainly like you better!

Speaking of magic, there is one word we SWCs consider the "magic word": *okay*. The word *okay* can work miracles. Using it helps a parent maintain authority while still sharing at least a portion of control. This "magic word" may not work with everyone, but it is usually effective more than 80 percent of the time with the SWC.

Consider this typical conversation:

"Tracy, put your seat belt on."

"No."

"I said, put your seat belt on."

"No."

Now what? She knows you can't drive and hold her seat belt on at the same time. You're facing a knock-down-drag-out power struggle with no winners.

"Fine! Then we're not going *anywhere*!"

Who just lost? That would be you. But what if you try this:

"Tracy, put your seat belt on, okay?"

"No."

"Why not?"

"It's too tight. I don't like it."

"Well, we'll loosen it a little, then put it on, okay?"

"Okay." Eight times out of ten this will be the response.

It's amazing but true—a small point of negotiation usually makes the difference.

"Sit down and don't move, okay?"

"No!"

"Why not?"

"I'm thirsty!"

"One quick drink, then sit down, okay?"

"Okay."

Asking, "Okay?" lets an SWC know that you realize she *does* always have a choice. Of course, *okay* doesn't mean "You don't have to do it." It means "You can choose the consequences if you want to," which leaves just enough control in the SWC's hands. You'll want to remember a couple of very important points here:

- Keep your voice firm and in control. If you seem weak or tentative, the SWC has to fight the urge to destroy you.

- You're not asking your SWC for permission. You're simply acknowledging he always has a choice—either to obey or to face the consequences.

4. Hand out more tickets; give fewer warnings.

During the training academy for my years as a police officer, we were instructed in what's called "violator contact." Part of the training describes this fourth strategy.

Let's say you make an illegal left turn and I pull you over in my patrol car. After I check to see that your driver's license and registration are valid and you have no outstanding warrants, there are two options: (1) I give you a ticket for the traffic violation you just committed, or (2) I give you a warning and spare you the expensive ticket.

Now let's suppose I decide to give you the warning instead of the ticket. You're anxious to get going, you're embarrassed at being pulled over, and you're impatient as I talk to you about why it's important not to disobey the traffic laws. As restless as you are, you must stay and listen to me for as long as I want to talk to you. After all, you're not getting a ticket, so this *is* your punishment.

But here's where it gets interesting, and at the academy we were given very specific instruction. If I decide to give you a ticket, I'm not supposed to give you a lecture or warning—just the ticket. It's one or the other, not both. This may surprise you, but most SWCs would rather, either figuratively or literally, have the ticket. Don't rant and rave and ask what lesson we have learned and shake your finger at us. Just write the ticket. Let me sign my name, pay my fine, and go calmly on with my life.

Now there is one more catch here. As a police officer, I can't get by with yelling, preaching, or shaking my finger at the offender when giving out the ticket. I need to keep my voice calm and professional, confident in my authority. This driver may choose to commit the same violation again or avoid paying the fine or ignore the court date. That's out of my control. It's my job to give the ticket, and I'll do it as many times as necessary.

Most SWCs will tell you we don't expect to be spared from the punishment we deserve. In fact, we know there will always be pain in order to gain—and an SWC will often calculate the cost of the ticket, and factor that into the decision whether or not to commit the violation. If you're anything like my mom, that may mystify you. When I was just three years old, my mom told me, "If you stand on that coffee table, I'm going to spank you." In my toddler head I was thinking, *How hard can that be? How long can that last?* So I climbed up on the coffee table and waited for the punishment I knew was coming. My mom was frustrated. You see, she thought if the punishment was unpleasant enough, I wouldn't do it. But it's not that simple.

Remember, we cannot allow you to take all control away from us; we always have a choice. You are not the final authority for determining whether or not we will comply—*we* are. So if you keep trying to find the one punishment that can *make* your child do what you want, there won't be a positive result for either you or your SWC.

As a parent, I learned the hard way—not only about the

fact that I wasn't the "big boss" but also about how I needed to phrase my demands in order to actually get my SWC to cooperate. I remember particularly one instance where I discovered why the "do it or else" tactic *doesn't* work.

"Michael Tobias, you need to pick up those toys and put them in the basket now!" Even as I heard myself issue the order to my then four-year-old, I realized I was in trouble. I sometimes forgot, and occasionally still forget, that Mike is just as strong willed as I am and that I have never reacted well to orders and ultimatums. But I had already climbed out on my limb, and I wasn't about to come back. Noting that Mike was not obeying, I moved a little farther out on the limb. "Mike, if I have to pick up those toys, I'm going to give them to other kids."

He stood as tall as he could and looked at me. "So give them to other kids," he said.

I couldn't hide my surprise. Among those toys were some of his favorites. But he'd just climbed out on his limb too. Without another word, I scooped up the toys and took them down to the garage. Later that week I gave them to the Compassionate Ministries program at our church. Almost twenty years later, Mike has still not asked what happened to any of those toys. He never asked to have any of them replaced. He knew what the price was, and he was fully prepared to pay it.

From the cradle to the grave, your SWC will present you

with challenges unlike those from your other children. The fact that you are the big person and your SWC is the small person is not enough to persuade her to cooperate. You cannot rule based on rank or privilege or even brute strength.

As the parent of an SWC, there's little doubt it's easier to give warnings than tickets. But it's also possible to give the warning or the ticket in a more positive way than the example I just gave you. What could I have done?

"Mike, as soon as you pick your toys up we'll go to Grandma's for ice cream, okay?"

"No. I don't want to pick up my toys."

"You don't want to go to Grandma's for ice cream?"

"Yes, but I don't want to pick up my toys."

"We'll leave in just a few minutes if the toys are picked up." Then I would leave the room.

A few minutes later, if I walked in and found the toys put away, we'd go to Grandma's. If the toys weren't put away, I would wait until Mike asked when we're going to Grandma's.

"We're not going to Grandma's, Mike. You didn't put your toys away."

Now many variations can happen in instances like this, but the point is, you communicate your authority by holding on to the bottom-line accountability. It works best if you can approach your SWC in a positive way, not a "you do it or else" way.

Parents frequently ask me for a list of tickets that will work for an SWC. But it's not that easy. Every SWC is unique, and you'll never find just one right ticket that works every time. You need to know your child, and it will take time and effort to figure out what works. When my boys were small, I figured out right away that Rob, my more compliant child, responded very well to time-out. But Mike? My SWC forced me to stand on the other side of the door, *holding* it shut the whole time-out. I quickly realized I was the only one being punished. That was not the right ticket.

For Mike, if a ticket was going to work at all, he responded much better to the loss of a privilege than to physical isolation. For Rob, because of his social nature, physical isolation was one of the best tickets ever. But I never did find the one right ticket for either boy that worked every time; they were always changing, which meant my approach needed to change as well.

Even though it's not always easy to come up with the ticket that will result in the behavior you're seeking in your SWC, one thing is sure. The SWC needs to know you're not going to keep giving warnings without getting around to delivering any consequences. We're looking for a lot less talk and a little more action on your part. Just stay calm and firm. If you're stuck for ideas on tickets, consider asking a good friend or family member who is an SWC. "I've got a kid who's a lot like you —can you tell me what might work?"

5. Make sure your SWC always knows your love is unconditional.

This point is so important it appears twice in this book—once as a key insight into understanding how SWCs think, and again here, in the top five list of critical strategies for bringing out the best in every SWC.

Demonstrating unconditional love can be challenging because we SWCs often don't make it easy for you to love us. Sometimes we experiment or make mistakes or even do outrageous things. When SWCs hear "I'll love you no matter what," we're almost always going to test it. *How about this? Do you love me now? What about this?* Sometimes it seems to us that you love us only if we do things your way and if we follow your rules. We don't expect you to let us get by with bad behavior, but we need to know that our relationship with you will stay intact no matter what.

One morning I happened to be watching a network news and talk show. Apparently the whole week had been devoted to stories about kids on drugs, exposing problems and offering solutions. This particular morning the show was promoting at-home drug test kits, and it featured a teenage boy who had been caught doing drugs. His parents were determined he would not get away with it.

The frightened and angry mother told the reporter how terrible the situation had been for her, and she quickly outlined a plan she and her husband had launched to turn their son around. Their tough-love contract was inflexible, and an at-home drug test would be ready at a moment's notice.

"I just can't believe he would do this to us! We raised him to be a good boy—we've always trusted him, and now *this*!" The camera panned from the distraught mother to her sullen thirteen-year-old son, the object of her anger and disappointment.

Although the camera focused on the mom's face, I watched her son in the background. As I studied his face, I couldn't help thinking he definitely knew he was in trouble. He knew he had made a big mistake. He knew he would have to pay some stiff penalties. Watching his face, though, what I *don't* think he knew was that his parents still loved him. You see, his mom didn't say, "We almost lost this boy, and he's so important to us. He's such a valuable part of our family, and we love him so much we'll do anything to bring him back. If it takes tough love, that's what we'll do. If we need to do drug tests, or even find a lockdown or rehabilitation program, we'll do it. We'll do whatever it takes, because we love him and we want him back."

But she didn't say that. She focused all of her attention on the behavior and how it reflected on her, not the relationship with her son. Meanwhile, her son slouched in the background with a posture and attitude somewhere between dejection and defiance. As the reporter wrapped up the segment, he turned the camera on the boy.

"Son," he said, "tell me, what do *you* think of all this?"

The teenager looked directly into the camera and said, "I can't wait to leave home."

As the shot faded, I kept thinking about that family. Did these parents really think it was worth it? By taking this heavy-handed approach, they were in danger of losing their son. Instead of bringing him back, they were driving him farther away. I don't believe they meant to do that. I think they honestly thought they were doing the best they could under the circumstances. But they overlooked a vital part of the solution: They had not fostered the kind of relationship with their son that he wanted to preserve.

Even when he *wasn't* annoying and disobeying them, did they still scold him? Had this boy's parents invested the time and effort it takes to let him know they really enjoyed having him around? When they taught him to do the right things, had they also noticed and appreciated the times he chose to follow their lead? If they had taken time to build the kind of relationship their son would value, their words of rebuke and harsh calls for change might have been effective. But if they had spent the last few years yelling at him more often than they spoke kindly to him, if they always seemed to notice what went wrong and simply said nothing when things went right, their son may have felt he essentially had nothing to lose. If his parents were going to yell and be mad at him no matter what, why should he even try? Most important, did their son have any concept at all of unconditional love?

I've heard many angry and frustrated parents assert that their SWC "has to learn to get along with the world." I gently remind them the jails are full of people who didn't *have* to get along with the world. Why not motivate your SWC to *want* to get along with the world in the first place? Then, if she has a strong and positive relationship with you, you'll be the one your child turns to for advice on how to do it.

I remember a particularly difficult day with my then-two-year-old SWC. I was certain he had spent the day irritating me on purpose. Just when I reached the end of my patience, he led me into the playroom. While I stood there, he crawled inside the empty toy cabinet and began to close the door. He leaned toward me and said loudly, "Go away!" Then he slammed the door. Although I secretly wanted to escape, I remained there. In a moment, the door flew open and I saw a startled, yet pleased, expression on his face. "You didn't go away!" he declared. Then he gave me a more serious look. "Go away!"

As we played the "go away, you didn't go away" game, I thought about how many SWCs, especially adolescents, tell their parents things like, "I hate you! Go away! Get out of my life! I never want to see you again!" Then they slam the door. I can tell you this for sure: inside they secretly, desperately hope you won't go away. They open the door, and you're still there. "I *told* you to go away! I *mean* it! I hate you! Leave me alone!" And they slam the door even harder. They wonder, *Did that do it? Did I really drive them away this time?*

Almost all of the SWCs I've talked to admit they often wonder whether their parents' love is truly unconditional. SWCs need to know there is nothing they can do that would actually make you stop loving them. They know there's a price to pay for making a wrong decision, but they have to know that losing your love will not be part of the cost. When SWCs feel secure in your love, you may be surprised at how seldom they test it.

◆ ◆ ◆

There you have it: Five to Thrive tips for working and living with the strong-willed child. Don't try to solve everything at once. Some tips will work better than others, but all of them will work to varying degrees, depending on the child, the day, the mood, and so on. Remember, hundreds of SWCs have endorsed these strategies, and hundreds more are out there just waiting for you to ask them for more ideas. It won't be as hard as you think!

But by shifting our focus from what we do
to what God does, don't we cancel out all
our careful keeping of the rules and ways
God commanded? Not at all. What happens,
in fact, is that by putting that entire way of life
in its proper place, we confirm it.

—Romans 3:31

4

What About the Line Between Right and Wrong?

How to Keep the SWC Accountable While Still Valuing Uniqueness

I once conducted an SWC seminar for a group of Christian radio advertising executives in the beautiful library of a grand Christian institution. As we discussed the characteristics of the SWC, Jay, one of the executives, leaped to his feet and grabbed the large family Bible that was close by.

"You're talking about the carnal nature!" he cried. "This strong-willed stuff is just sin, pure and simple!" The rest of us were surprised at his intensity.

"Whoa!" I said quickly. "Sin comes in all styles and sizes. No one personality or learning style has a corner on anything good or anything bad." He shook his head, still holding the big black Bible.

"But you're supposed to obey," he protested. "God doesn't compromise and negotiate and let you off the hook just because you don't want to follow the rules!"

I nodded. "You're right. He doesn't. But God is the One who designed us with a free will in the first place. Doesn't it stand to reason that He would work within His own parameters? I believe God wants to use the strong will He placed in so many of us. Sin is still sin, whether it is being committed by a compliant person or a strong-willed person. Strong will is not the issue. The issue is the line between what's right and wrong."

Jay did not look completely convinced. One of his SWC colleagues chimed in, "Jay, I don't work the way you do at all, but both of us are successful at our jobs. I know my strong will gets me in trouble sometimes, and I have to make things right, both with God and the person I wronged. But you've gotten in trouble once in a while too, even though you're not the classic strong-willed child!"

Jay nodded and started to smile. "Yeah. Actually, I got in trouble because I came across as being too rigid and inflexible to accept my client's wild ideas." He put the Bible down and took his seat again. "Okay, I get your point. But I still think you strong-willed folks sin a lot more often than I do." He was grinning as the guy next to him jabbed an elbow into Jay's ribs.

Contrary to what some popular theories propose, I believe (as do most SWCs I've talked to) that there *are* moral absolutes. I don't ascribe to the idea of right and wrong being relative. However, it's especially difficult for SWCs to get along with those who think they are the only ones qualified to define right and wrong.

Parents and teachers often tell me they believe SWCs delight in breaking rules and getting away with doing wrong things. That's not an SWC trait. That's sin, and anyone— strong willed or not—can do that. Again, let me take you into the mind of an SWC when it comes to following the rules.

Rules are basically guidelines.

For those who believe it's important not to rock the boat, or who accept what traditionally works, the actions of the SWC can look suspiciously like disobedience and rebellion. To most SWCs, rules are basically guidelines. It's not arrogance on our part—we just believe we're capable of figuring out what the point of a rule is, and sometimes we use another method of accomplishing that goal.

For example, if I drive into the school parking lot for an evening PTA meeting and the closest parking places are marked "Bus Zone—No Parking," I interpret that sign to mean, "If the buses need these spaces, you can't park here. However, if the buses don't need them, you can park here." It's a guideline! On the other hand, you won't find a stronger advocate than I am when it comes to making sure "Handicapped Only" parking is strictly enforced twenty-four hours a day. The reason behind that particular rule is sound, and I don't consider the issue negotiable.

Another good example has now become my classic "stroller story." I first told the story in my book *The Way They Learn*. My rule-conscious sister Sandee and I were shopping in a department store a few years ago. Sandee's youngest daughter, Allison, was still a toddler, and we had her in a stroller. As we got ready to go to the second floor in the store, I took charge of the stroller and approached the escalator. "Wait!" Sandee cried. "Look at that sign! It says 'No Strollers on the Escalator.'"

I stared at her. "Are the stroller police going to arrest me?" I asked. "Sandee, that sign is for people who don't know how to safely *put* a stroller on an escalator. Since I *do,* it doesn't apply to me." I swiftly took Allison out and held her securely in my arms as the empty stroller rode beside me up the escalator. My sister did not even follow me for a few minutes. She was horrified that I would so blatantly disregard a rule. But to me, it was simply a guideline. The point was to keep the child safe, and I absolutely accomplished that.

A few weeks later, I found out I wasn't the only one who interpreted the stroller policy this way. As I descended a Dallas/

Fort Worth airport escalator, I noticed a young couple ascending with a huge baby buggy. Even from a distance, I could tell the wife was reading her husband the riot act for bringing the prohibited buggy on the escalator. As I passed them, I heard the husband say to his wife, "Did anybody die? Nobody died!"

As parents, we can't give SWCs permission to break a rule. But I can tell you rule breaking is bound to happen, and your reaction is so important. When you set parameters for the behavior of an SWC, it helps to be clear with your reasons for rules and regulations. We don't usually set out to break rules just out of meanness. Sometimes, though, we end up breaking rules or disobeying because we feel we have no other choice. Perhaps the rule seems pointless. Perhaps the result of obeying will hurt someone else or compromise our beliefs. Perhaps the restrictions seem designed to simply let another person exercise power over us. If you become heavy-handed in your approach and start issuing orders to be obeyed, everyone is headed for trouble.

For most SWCs, the issue of right and wrong isn't tied to a specific religion or belief system as much as it's an inherent part of who we are. Deep inside, we want to do the right thing, and we often fight on behalf of others who aren't able to stand up against injustice on their own. But the same strong spirit that can make us champions of the truth can also create in us a strong resistance to those who think they have ultimate authority.

When you work with your SWC on issues of discipline or

correction, your reaction to the situation and what you say and do can make all the difference in the world. Let's look at three scenarios that demonstrate how a parent's carefully chosen reaction not only can avoid a crisis, but also can reinforce strong, positive values.

1. Your SWC doesn't want to go to church.

Eleven-year-old Kelsey made the announcement calmly at the breakfast table on Sunday morning. "I'm not going to go to church anymore."

Her mother's reaction was swift and disbelieving. "What? You most certainly are going, young lady. Your father is the pastor, for heaven's sake!"

Kelsey's dad looked at her thoughtfully before he spoke. "Kelsey, why don't you want to go to church?"

She shrugged. "I just don't. There's nothing to do. It's boring and I'm tired of it."

"Sometimes I feel that way too." At his daughter's look of surprise, Kelsey's dad continued. "We all get a bit tired of the routine sometimes. But the whole point of going to church is to learn more about God and to spend time with others who want to do the same. Tell me, what do you think would motivate you to want to go to church again?"

"I don't know," she replied.

Her dad scooted his chair closer to her. "Kelsey, what about going to church today and, instead of listening, you write notes about what you think might make things more interesting. There are probably other kids who feel like you do, and you may be able to come up with some great ideas for making church better for everyone."

Kelsey was intrigued in spite of herself. "Well," she said, "I think I know some things that would make Sunday a lot more fun."

"Good!" her dad exclaimed. "I'm encouraged already. I think you'll be a great source of ideas for us."

Kelsey stood up and looked around. "Do you know where I could find some paper and a pen?" Her mother was already bringing the necessary supplies.

If your SWC suddenly decides he is no longer going to go to church with you, don't react in anger, and don't force the issue. Try to find out why your SWC doesn't want to go—but don't ask impatiently. When you ask why, your SWC may not really know or may not be able to put his feelings into words. Try asking things like "What would motivate you to want to go?" or "What do you think the point of going to church should be?" Make a concerted effort to listen to your SWC's responses. The answers will almost certainly reveal more than you anticipate. Your SWC needs to feel he has input. The more you can involve your SWC in coming up with the solution, the better your chances of avoiding the problem in the first place.

2. Your SWC expresses doubts about your church, your beliefs, or your values.

"Everybody cheats a little, Dad."

Max looked at his eighteen-year-old SWC in amazement. "What in the world would make you say a thing like that? You know we don't condone that sort of behavior."

David retorted, "Yeah, well, we don't have much money either."

Max struggled to control his anger. "Son, you know we've always had enough, and we make our money honestly."

"But, Dad," David frowned, "it's not like we have to become crooks or anything. It's called creative financing."

Max sat down across the table from his son. "Listen, David, I know it's appealing to make a lot of money quickly, even if you have to cheat just a little to do it. I know a lot of people get by with it. But your mother and I have always found that we sleep better knowing we have nothing to hide, no one to fear. It's kept our whole family healthy and happy. If you decide to take a different path, that will be your choice, but investigate it carefully. See if the folks you are following down that road are anywhere near as happy together as your mom and I are."

David looked exasperated. "Dad, that's so corny."

"I agree. But all I ask is that you check into what you are doing very carefully. I know you want to make money, and I'll help you as much as I can. But I want to do it the old-fashioned way. Let's give it a try my way first, okay?"

David hesitated. "Well, I'm not making any promises; but I'd never expect you to cheat."

Max grinned. "That's a start, son. That's a start."

When your SWC has doubts about what you believe and taught him all his life, it's usually best to meet the issues head-on and face the questions honestly. You don't need to provide all the answers, but your relationship will be strengthened if you empathize with his need to find them. He doesn't want to feel he's doing something horribly wrong if he expresses doubts about what he believes. You can be an understanding guide, provide the Bible as a guidebook, and help your SWC enjoy the journey of discovering who he will be and what he will stand for.

3. Your SWC has turned completely away from God and totally rejects your views.

My friend Pat struggled for years with her wayward teenage son. Ray had always been a rebel, and as soon as he graduated from high school, he left home and revealed his addiction to drugs and alcohol. Pat and her husband were heartbroken and more than a little discouraged, but they never gave up praying that Ray would change his ways and come home.

I ran into Pat a few years ago and asked about her son. Her

face became absolutely radiant. "Ray's home!" she said happily. "He's a new man! I've got my wonderful boy again." I asked her what changed him, and she smiled. "That's the best part," she declared. "Ray said it wasn't anything we actually told him. He said he just kept remembering all those nights after he went to bed when he heard his dad and me praying for him and thanking God for giving us a son like Ray. He told me it was because we never really preached at him or made him feel he had to be a certain way in order for us to love him. He said when he felt like he had reached the bottom and had nowhere to go, he remembered what a great place home would be if he could just get there again."

If you have a prodigal son or daughter, you'll experience many challenges and moments of pain and sadness. But don't panic. Stay calm and loving, and do a lot of praying. In the end your SWC needs to have a safe place to come home to and a reason to return. If he knows he'll be assaulted with words of recrimination and reminders of where he went wrong, he'll probably do everything he can to avoid you. If, on the other hand, he knows he will always find you praying for him, loving him, and keeping a place open at the table, he knows he has something to come back to. As hard as it is to stay focused, keep asking yourself, "Why would my SWC want to come back?" Make sure your answers are appealing!

It all comes back to relationship.

When I ask SWCs who are dedicated Christians what motivated them to surrender their lives to God, I get one consistent answer: We are motivated by the relationship God offers us, not by the punishment we can avoid. In other words, it doesn't work to tell us that unless we surrender to God, we will face eternal damnation or hell. In fact, this approach may drive us farther away.

What attracts the SWC to God is the relationship and the opportunity to be loved and understood by the One who knows us best. Many parents are justifiably concerned about the eternal well-being of their SWC. It may seem as if their child is trying to get as far away from God and the established church as possible. In spite of good intentions, parents may put too much pressure on their SWCs to conform to what they believe to be true. The SWC sees ways to be valuable and unique in serving a personally accessible God. God wants each of us to come to Him and to serve Him in a way that enhances the very personality He created within us.

Every SWC needs to know that God is not simply a narrow, dictatorial authority who offers no choices or alternatives. God does, however, demand obedience. And He certainly has drawn a clear line between right and wrong. In Proverbs 3:5 the Bible states, "Trust in the LORD with all your heart and lean not on your own understanding" (NIV). I believe that means I don't have a corner on understanding. There may be many approaches, many styles, and many ways besides mine. But verse 6 holds me accountable to a higher authority: "In all your ways acknowledge him" (NIV). I believe that means that as long as I'm using my style and unique personality to bring honor and glory to God, it's okay—I'm on the right track. But if I use them in a way that does *not* acknowledge or bring glory to God, it's not okay, no matter what style I am. That's the bottom line. That's the line that can't be crossed.

I was working at a large Christian school, taking the high school sophomores through a workbook to help them understand their individual learning style strengths. One of the teachers had warned me about Brad, a particularly strong-willed student who seemed to always be pushing the boundaries and causing a lot of trouble. Sure enough, Brad was first to raise his hand after figuring out his learning style profile and completing his "strong-will" checklist.

"See?" he said loudly. "This is just who I am. I shouldn't have to follow a bunch of stupid rules or dress codes when I'm designed by God to be a free spirit!"

I smiled and walked toward him. "May I ask you just one thing, Brad?"

He nodded and said, "Sure."

I pointed to the scripture written on the board: Proverbs 3:5–6. "How does what you're saying square up with this?"

The triumphant smile disappeared from his face, and he shrugged his shoulders. "I guess I see your point," he admitted. Instead of engaging Brad in an argument, I had the opportunity to lead the whole class in a very lively and positive discussion for a few minutes before moving on to the next subject.

I love hearing Steve Green, a contemporary Christian music artist, sing one of my favorite songs, "Find Us Faithful." As an SWC whose greatest motivation has always come by way of love and inspiration, I find the chorus especially meaningful:

> May all who come behind us
> Find us faithful;
> May the fire of our devotion light their way.
> May the footprints that we leave
> Lead them to believe—
> And the lives we live
> Inspire them to obey.[1]

In a nutshell:

- If you want to motivate me, inspire me.
- If you want to direct me, lead the way.
- If you want to encourage my ambition, ignite the fire with your enthusiasm.

Do you want to be counted wise,

to build a reputation for wisdom?

Here's what you do:

Live well, live wisely, live humbly.

It's the way you live,

not the way you talk,

that counts.

—James 3:13

5

So What's the Big Deal About School?

Great Information for Helping an SWC Succeed in School

"Do I have to do this assignment?" The question came from a notoriously strong-willed student with a reputation for being a troublemaker. Her eyes flashed an unmistakable challenge: *Just try and make me.*

I gave her a casual glance. "No," I replied. "You don't have to do it."

She couldn't hide her surprise. "You mean I get an A and I don't have to do it?" she asked incredulously.

"No." I shook my head. "You get an F. But you don't have to do it."

She frowned, shrugged her shoulders, and went back to her seat. In moments, she had begun to work on the assignment.

She just wanted to let me know she could get an F if she wanted to. That's right. She always has a choice.

The years I spent as a high-school teacher brought me hundreds of students who were labeled troublemakers, smart alecks, and worse. Frankly, they were usually my favorite kids. They were bright, intuitive, creative, and just a bit obnoxious. They thought school was boring. So did I, and I was the teacher! They asked blunt questions like, "Why are we doing this?" and "Why can't I do it a different way?" They loudly complained that homework was a waste of time and life was too short for boring, repetitive drills. Those kids were inconvenient, but they also kept me on my toes.

Every summer vacation during the eight years I taught in the public schools, I went back to work in the corporate world. I did it not only for extra income but also for the diverse experience. I wanted to know if I was effectively preparing my students for the world after graduation. That first summer, I made a startling discovery: In the real world, you get hired for the things that got you in trouble in school.

Think about it. Most employers are looking for someone with good social interaction, a high energy level, and independent thinking skills. We not only don't foster those traits in school, we often actively *discourage* them. And yet many highly successful people struggled with the traditional classroom demands and were labeled "inconvenient" at best, "disciplinary problems" at worst. Ask a busy entrepreneur, a top-producing salesperson, or a talented actor about grades achieved in school, and you'll often find they don't even want to talk about it.

For many SWCs, school seems like a prison sentence, a punishment to be endured. From our SWC perspective, so much of school is drill, repetition, and endless busywork that it isn't worth the trouble to get good grades. Many parents face a great dilemma in motivating their SWC for academic achievement. Every child is gifted in unique and valuable ways. Every child possesses intelligence and potential for success. But sometimes an SWC's greatest strengths aren't appreciated in the classroom.

I'd like to offer a few insights into why SWCs may make life difficult for our parents and teachers when it comes to academics and classroom behavior.

Just because we can get an A doesn't mean we want to.

I read an interesting article a few years ago written by some excited researchers who claimed they had finally proven that every human brain is capable of mastering advanced calculus. I remember thinking, *But why would I want to?*

It's hard for some parents to accept the fact their SWC would actually be willing to settle for a lower grade than he is capable of achieving. But remember, you can't *make* him want a better grade, and he might just decide it isn't worth the effort. Very frustrating, I know, but often the more emphasis you put on the grade, the more you may find your SWC determined not to cooperate. What if your SWC's grades don't reflect what's actually been learned? For some, it's enough to know how good grades can affect scholarships and future opportunities, but for other SWCs if you make grades the goal, it will backfire on you almost every time.

Jason's mom was at the end of her rope. Her sixteen-year-old SWC was flunking out of his economics class, and she told me she'd tried everything to get him to improve the grade: threats, promises, bribes. "Jason can ace that class," she insisted, "but he won't even try!"

I knew enough about Jason's mom to have a good idea what the real problem was. She was a smart lady herself, one of those students who got straight As in school. She knew her son was intelligent, and she couldn't understand why he wouldn't exert the effort to get a good grade. I also knew Jason well enough to recognize that he was exhibiting a classic SWC behavior. Why spend valuable time studying for a class that he would have no use for in the future?

I asked his mom a couple questions. "Does Jason need this class to graduate?"

"No," she admitted. "But a failing grade sure won't look good to the college he has decided he wants to attend."

"Have you asked Jason what grade he wants to get in this class?"

She looked surprised. She had never considered working for less than an A in any class. As we talked, Jason's mom forced herself to consider my SWC advice. Here's what worked:

Jason's mom made sure her son knew the point of taking this class in the first place. He agreed that he wanted to keep his transcript looking good for his college applications, something he hadn't considered in his attitude toward this class. He admitted that a D or an F would look pretty bad. His mom asked if he'd want to work for at least a C, knowing that a C figured into his grade-point average wouldn't kill his chances for future scholarships.

She suggested Jason ask his economics teacher what he would have to do in order to get a C by the end of the semester. Jason felt relieved. He knew he wasn't motivated to work for an A in that class. But a C—well, he could do that without very much effort. His mom, his teacher, and Jason briefly designed a strategy for getting the C, and he went to work.

The pressure for getting an A was off. The point of taking the class was clear. In the end, Jason actually got a B instead of a C, and he admitted he enjoyed the challenge.

If your SWC refuses to do homework, maybe homework isn't the issue.

How many battles have you fought with your SWC over homework? We SWCs don't relish the thought of doing more schoolwork after we've left the classroom. The idea that we must also devote our spare time to doing something we could barely endure all day long seems ridiculous. If you assume we should do the homework just because it's assigned, you'll have a battle on your hands almost every time. Remember, your SWC needs an answer to the question "What's the point?"

SWCs want to know why we should spend time and effort doing something. We're not just being smart alecks. We truly want to know the answer to the question. If we understand the purpose of the homework (and sometimes the explanation can be as simple as "It's just a necessary hoop to jump through"), we can make a conscious decision as to whether it's worth our efforts to do it.

Remember, SWCs know there are consequences for not doing homework, but we also believe we can choose to take the consequences. As much as a parent may not want to think about this, the fact is you cannot force your SWC to do the homework. We can be motivated, inspired, and held accountable, but we cannot be forced to do homework against our will. Many parents end up doing the work themselves. Some yell and scream and punish, but almost all those parents end up being the ones who suffer the most. *Your* high blood pressure, *your* headaches, *your* ulcers won't help an SWC get the homework done.

So what can you do? Here are some suggestions:

1. Establish the reason for doing homework in the first place.

Your SWC will respect the fact that you're as honest as possible in evaluating the purpose. Let's face it: Sometimes homework is a waste of time. It can be boring, repetitious busywork. But the reality is that—right or wrong—often the homework assignments are counted as part of the student's final grade. Help your SWC figure out what needs to be done in order to accomplish the goal he sets.

Jason, for example, had determined he wanted to get at least a C in his economics class. If doing a certain amount of homework is part of the equation, he'll need to know that the consequences for not doing his homework could be that he loses the C. Then he decides whether or not it's worth doing.

2. If grades themselves are not a motivating factor, find out what is.

Obviously each SWC will be different. For instance, the practice spelling tests and sentence drills were a pain in the neck for my second-grade SWC. He felt he already knew the words, and if he missed a couple, well, they probably weren't that important anyway. The evenings at home were becoming tense and full of arguments as Mike kept putting off his homework. Finally, I took some of my own advice. I know Mike loves checklists and charts. I asked him to help me design a chart for keeping track of finished tasks each week. One of those tasks was studying for his spelling test. He loved checking off the items on the chart, and soon he rarely had an unfinished assignment!

If your SWC is not a chart person, experiment with other motivators. It may take some time and a few failed experiments to find an approach that works. For older kids, it works best to let them figure out on their own what motivates them. Ask them questions like, "What do you think it will take?" or, "How will we know it's working?" If they just can't think of anything, ask before you give unsolicited advice. "Would you like me to give you a suggestion?" If the answer is no, just drop the subject for a while and come back to it later. If the answer is yes, you'll know your input is actually welcome.

3. Keep a calm, reasonable attitude as much as possible.

Whenever you can, phrase your requirements in the form of positive rather than negative terms. For example, instead of saying, "If you don't get that homework done by dinner, you won't be watching your favorite television show tonight!" try saying,

"Your favorite TV show is on at eight. You'll need to have your homework done before that so you won't miss any of it."

4. Put as much control as you can into the hands of your SWC.

Let your child know what the point of the homework is and what the consequences of not doing it will be, and then let him decide what to do. You may sometimes have to back off and let your SWC accept the consequences without rescuing him at the last minute. When children realize they really will be held accountable, they can change their perspective and begin to take responsibility for themselves instead of relying on their parents to rescue them.

Help your SWC maintain a good relationship with teachers.

Earlier, we discussed the importance of a good relationship between parents and SWCs. This fundamental concept is just as important when it comes to the teacher-student interaction. Even teachers who are perceived as boring or uncreative and predictable can still have a positive influence on an SWC if they truly love and value the child.

Respect is definitely a two-way street. If the teacher recognizes and appreciates the strengths of an SWC, that SWC probably won't pose much of a discipline problem. But when a teacher fails to appreciate individual strengths or insists on a rigid and inflexible code of conduct, trouble begins. Here's a classic example:

> Josh was a fun-loving SWC in the third grade. His teacher, Mrs. Jones, was strict—a by-the-book discipli-narian. One afternoon during recess, a mischief-maker turned every student's desk to face the back of the room. When Mrs. Jones and her class came in, she immedi-ately issued the command, "All right, children, I want you to turn your desks around at once." Every child ex-cept Josh quickly turned his desk to face the front of the room again.
>
> Josh, after pausing a moment, turned his desk around—all the way around—and sat with his back to the teacher. Mrs. Jones could have quickly diffused the situation if she really understood how Josh's mind works. She could have said something like, "Oh, that's cute, Josh. Nice to see your back," and gone on teach-ing. It would only take a few moments while Josh was getting a couple laughs for him to turn his desk around and join the rest of the class. Unfortunately, that's not how it went down.
>
> Mrs. Jones was furious. She pointed her finger at

Josh and said, "That's enough, young man! You turn your desk around and face me this instant or you are on your way to the principal's office!" The ultimatum had been issued, and Josh simply shrugged and walked out of the room and toward the principal's office.

I'm not advocating that teachers let kids get by with smart-mouth or inappropriate comments. But Josh wasn't trying to be disrespectful. He struggled all year with the fact that Mrs. Jones never seemed to appreciate his sense of humor. He knew how to push her buttons, and she repaid him with nothing but anger and punishment. It didn't have to be that way.

Contrast Josh's experience with that of Katherine, a troubled thirteen-year-old SWC who had barely survived her parents' divorce. She was a pretty good kid, but adolescence hit her hard. Junior high was dramatically different from elementary school, and the mix of home problems and new social circumstances was proving to be too much. She began to experiment with a little alcohol, and a few drugs. Her mom was frantic but was struggling to keep her own life together.

Katherine began to spiral out of control. Her grades plummeted, her choice of friends caused her family distress, and she defied her mother at every turn. Enter Mrs. Adams. This quiet, unassuming junior high school teacher truly loved kids. Right away she spotted Katherine and made her a special project.

Katherine told me a few years later that Mrs. Adams made all the difference in the world when it came to school survival. Here was a teacher who was a tough disciplinarian, who held her students to a high academic standard, and who could motivate Katherine to do whatever she asked her to do.

Why? Mrs. Adams told Katherine how much she loved the way her mind was wired. She looked for ways Katherine could be successful without having to conform to traditional methods. She commiserated with Katherine about some of the class requirements that seemed boring or irrelevant. Katherine told me how much it meant to know that Mrs. Adams would hold her accountable but would never embarrass her or make her feel small.

Katherine began to stay after school voluntarily, helping Mrs. Adams and talking to her for hours. And because Mrs. Adams was firm about getting work out of the way before enjoying any leisure time, Katherine actually did her homework. Katherine usually didn't want to go home, but Mrs. Adams would gently nudge her out, telling her how much she looked forward to seeing her the next day. By the end of ninth grade, Katherine had decided she wanted to be a teacher, and Mrs. Adams was already helping her plan a strategy for succeeding in college and beginning her career.

When I met Katherine a few years ago, she was in her fourth year of teaching seventh- and eighth-grade math. She said she loved teaching, but she especially loved getting all the kids that none of the other teachers wanted. She winked and said, "I think Mrs. Adams would have liked it that way too!"

So how can you get a teacher for your SWC who's more like Mrs. Adams than Mrs. Jones? There are no guarantees, but you have more control than you may think. Despite a lot of bad press about teachers, you'll find that many of them truly love kids. There are more demands on a teacher's time and curriculum than ever before, so if you want to help your SWC really get to know her teacher and be known, you and your child will need to do most of the legwork. Here are two things you can do.

1. Write a brief profile of your SWC, listing natural strengths and abilities.

When you talk to your child's teacher, ask how you and your SWC can help use those strengths to succeed in the classroom. Don't list or dwell on limitations or shortcomings. Your child already knows what she doesn't do well. Start with and emphasize the positive aspects, and encourage the teacher to help you design ways to overcome challenges in the classroom.

2. Keep an open line of communication between you, your SWC, and the teacher.

Encourage your SWC to speak to the teacher every day, even if it's just to say hello and make mention of something positive.

("I like the new poster." "That's a cool necklace." "I'm glad you gave us an extra day for the test.") It won't take long for the teacher to begin to notice your child and start making positive comments in return. Drop a personal note to the teacher every once in a while, reinforcing how much you appreciate her efforts to help kids learn and feel valued. Let the teacher know that you aren't going to let your SWC get by with excuses for not doing work or obeying the rules, but that you also want to find as many ways as possible to help your child succeed.

Your SWC will watch your relationship with his teacher carefully. If you make it a priority to maintain a good one, the chances are much better the SWC will follow your example. If you do get into a position where you believe a teacher will simply not be flexible or accepting of your SWC's strengths, you may need to pursue a course that would allow your SWC to change teachers or classroom situations. (For a more detailed explanation of how to do this, read chapter 8 of my book *Every Child Can Succeed*.)

What if the teacher thinks your child has a learning disability?

You know by now that the SWC doesn't fit any particular mold or follow a predictable pattern. SWCs often thrive on change and conflict, and we may have a completely different perspective than the average person. We present you with some unique challenges, but we can also provide you with some wonderful insights and innovations. Boredom can be our greatest enemy. We have to keep things moving, changing, interesting. The longer we're left on our own to simply sit quietly and listen, the greater the chance for us to get in trouble. You can see why the benefits of an SWC's unique perspective get overlooked when the education system insists that the student be the only one who adjusts and accommodates.

When the SWC resists, he may be tested for learning disabilities or behavior disorders, such as ODD (oppositional defiant disorder). But what if the very traits and characteristics that get the SWC in trouble are the ones that could potentially change the world? A few years ago, psychiatrist and medical expert Peter R. Breggin, MD, quoted *Newsweek* magazine in his book *The War Against Children*. Dr. Breggin said that *Newsweek* had asked the questions, "Where do great minds come from? And why are there no Einsteins, Freuds or Picassos today?"[1] Dr. Breggin then responded with a sobering thought: "What if we're medicating them?"[2]

When you think about it, all three of those great men would have fit most, if not all, of the symptoms of many learning disorders. Attention deficit disorder (A.D.D.) is being diagnosed more rapidly than most parents and schools can dispense the daily dose of medication. The at-risk programs in many school districts are overflowing with candidates who are unsuccessful in the regular classroom. More and more, students are participating in pull-out programs, where they must leave the classroom to get individual or specialized help. Certainly, legitimate physiological and neurological disorders exist. However, if a child with a bona fide disability is placed with ten other children who simply have exhibited inconvenient or downright bad behavior, that child will not receive the help he truly needs. (You'll find some helpful resources in the bibliography at the end of this book.)

Perhaps we need to ask ourselves an important question: If this many kids can't cope with the traditional classroom, shouldn't we be changing the classroom instead of just trying to change the kids? I'm not talking about special privileges or dumbing down the system. I'm talking about deciding what the point of education is, and then finding effective ways to achieve the goal. It's not really such a mystery. In his book *Teaching Through Encouragement,* Robert Martin put forth a simple but profound explanation for why children may not be paying attention: "Inattention is really a way of saying that a student is paying attention to something the teacher isn't interested in. A student who never pays attention is paying attention to something."[3]

If your SWC thinks school is boring and hates doing work

that seems to have no point or purpose, is it surprising that she may become a candidate for special education? Might it be that her disinterest doesn't have anything to do with a lack of intelligence or even a lack of ability?

The blame, of course, can't be laid solely at the educators' feet. Nor can we assume that a child's difficulty is due to a lack of motivation or failure to match learning styles. There are no pat formulas that will give us quick answers to the question of why an SWC is not doing well in school. But it's important that we don't assume our child's unconventional behaviors or learning styles are indicative of a disability. It's essential that we determine how much of our SWC's lack of success may be due to a physical, psychological, or educational disorder issue and how much may be due to the system's failure to recognize and value the way her mind works.

You can be your SWC's greatest advocate for getting the best possible education. You know your child. Help your child's teacher recognize and understand your child's strengths. Don't throw your hands up and surrender when the school wants to label your SWC. Stay positive, but be firm. If you believe your child needs to be evaluated for a learning disability, by all means follow a cautious path. A well-versed pediatrician can help you rule out physical problems first. The doctor can then assist you in finding trustworthy counselors or educators to evaluate the symptoms and find out how much is a matter of learning style and how much goes beyond that.

Keep an open mind, and search until you find a medical professional you can trust, preferably one who has a handle on the differences in learning styles and recognizes the hallmark traits of an SWC. It can make a huge difference when you pull down the lines of first resistance before you take more drastic action.

You cannot excuse bad behavior; you cannot allow disruptive activity; you must not let your SWC get by on special exemptions or privileges. By the same token, you dare not assume that something is inherently wrong with your SWC because he will not do things your way, or that his brain is "broken" because of a poor fit between student and classroom.

Keep school in perspective.

Next time you find yourself arguing with your SWC over homework, grades, and tests, ask yourself how important the whole issue will be ten years from now. Ask yourself some questions: What is the real issue, getting the job done or getting things done your way? Is it worth sacrificing your relationship? Does your SWC know the point?

If you can identify and use your SWC's natural strengths,

you'll find that success may be more attainable than you thought—in school and in life! (In addition to the resources at the back of the book, you can go to www.AppleSt.com to find free learning style profiles to use with your children.)

Make a careful exploration of who you are

and the work you have been given,

and then sink yourself into that.

Don't be impressed with yourself.

Don't compare yourself with others.

Each of you must take responsibility

for doing the creative best you can

with your own life.

—Galatians 6:4–5

6

How Can I Help a Strong-Willed Child Find the Right Career?

Guiding SWCs Toward Using Their Strengths in the Future

I was young and enthusiastic when I started my student-teaching position at a suburban high school. I was so excited about spending time with actual students it didn't occur to me other teachers might not share my zeal. My first day of lunch in the teachers' lounge caught me completely by surprise.

As I sat with some of those seasoned professionals, I expected to overhear pearls of wisdom, bits of advice, and voices of experience. Instead, I heard several murmurs of discontent about the "system" and more than a few complaints about specific students and classroom conditions. One middle-aged teacher stood up to refill his coffee cup. "I hate the whole system," he groused. "I hate the kids and I hate the paperwork, and I especially hate the new training requirements."

I didn't know enough to keep quiet, so I let my incredulous expression show when I spoke to him. I wasn't being impertinent, but I wanted to ask him an important question. "If you hate teaching so much," I said, "why don't you quit and do something you like?"

It was his turn to be surprised. He gave me a contemptuous look. "You're just a rookie," he snorted. "You'll catch on. I'm forty-five years old and I'm vested in the retirement system. I've got steady pay, time off in the summer, and health benefits for my family. Why would I want to start all over now?"

I didn't reply, but it was a clarifying moment. Suddenly I realized how vital it was that I never feel trapped in a job. I vowed I would not allow myself to focus on my career so narrowly that I couldn't leave when I stopped being passionate about what I was doing.

The jobs I held each summer while I was teaching were usually through a temporary employment agency. I honed my secretarial abilities and began learning new skills by volunteering for a wide variety of jobs. I worked as a statistical typist for a trucking company, as a marketing assistant for a large advertising agency, as an inventory taker for a gaming company, and as a driver for a limousine-rental company. I held a variety of positions until I landed in my favorite temp job—six years as a fully-commissioned reserve police officer. All of those experiences prepared me well for my successful and fulfilling career as a writer and speaker.

Over the next several years, I was able to tell every new class of students the same thing at the beginning of each school year. "I could be a lot of different places, doing a lot of different things. I'm here teaching you because I want to be here more than anywhere else. As soon as I want to be somewhere else more than I want to be here, I owe it to you and to myself to leave."

After eight years of teaching high school, the day came when I realized that it was time to make a difference by teaching teachers. It was a step of faith when I went into business for myself, but it's one of the most fulfilling things I've ever done.

I have since found that most of my SWC friends and colleagues share my perspective on work. Something in our nature makes us chafe with restlessness when we feel trapped by a job that bores or frustrates us. Work is not simply an obligation we fulfill or a duty we carry out because we must put food on the table. We need to be compelled, fulfilled, challenged.

If you're not an SWC, this may sound unrealistic to you. You may insist that SWCs need to "get a grip" and "learn to live in the real world." After all, what are the chances that your SWC could actually get that perfect job? Well, what if it could happen?

Wouldn't you rather prepare your SWC to get the job of his dreams than prepare him to settle for whatever he can get?

I was once a guest on a call-in radio show in upstate New York. We had been talking about a variety of ways kids don't fit in school, especially the highly active and extremely restless SWC. I strongly advocated directing the SWC's high energy level instead of trying to squelch it. One irate caller disagreed. "My second-grade daughter is on the move all the time," he said. "I make her be still because I tell her that someday she's going to have a job where she can't just move around any time she wants to."

"Sir, are you calling me from work right now?" I asked.

"Yes," he replied.

"Where are you calling me from?" I inquired.

There was a moment's pause before he answered. "My truck. Never mind—I get your point."

Why do we think our SWCs will be destined to work in careers they don't like and that don't suit them? Certainly we need to train our children to stretch outside their comfort zones and be disciplined enough to do things they may not particularly enjoy. But why don't we spend more time helping them discover what they are naturally drawn to and what they can do that will truly be enjoyable for them?

There are many ways to identify and appreciate which strengths will be most appropriate for possible careers in your

SWC's future. The common denominator seems to be summed up in one word: diversification. SWCs thrive when we have lots of options, so it stands to reason the best preparation for adulthood will be to help your SWC learn a variety of skills, explore multiple job opportunities, and conquer many challenges. It's never too early to begin, and as many recent career-search books and websites can verify, it's never too late to start. Let's take a look at some practical ways you can help your SWC discover his future interests, from early childhood through the teen years.

Prepare them for the rest of their lives.

Early childhood

Encourage exploration from the beginning. Let your SWC wander freely among the possibilities and show you what naturally captures her interest.

When our boys were toddlers, they stayed at Grandma's house every day while I worked. Although they were barely walking and talking, we noticed they had a real thirst for knowledge, and they were curious about everything. But the twins were already so different from each other we didn't want to insist they both always do the same thing. So we went to an educational-supplies store and bought several inexpensive posters featuring days of the week, months of the year, animal alphabets, the solar system, neighborhood helpers, and other topics. We posted the charts throughout Grandma's house at eye level for the boys.

Over the next few weeks we watched the boys and answered their questions. Each boy would approach one of the charts, point, and say, "What's that?" We would tell him, and then he would either pursue more questions or walk away without further interest. We applied no pressure for them to learn what was on the posters, yet both boys eagerly wanted to learn. Robert was drawn to neighborhood helpers and to other people-oriented charts. Mike, on the other hand, focused carefully on the solar system and on categorizing the months in a year. We were setting the stage for encouraging the boys to pursue their interests instead of simply enduring a uniform, prescribed routine.

You may want to start keeping a journal to share with your child when she is older. Even if you only jot down a few things once a week, this is a great way to track your SWC's likes and dislikes, interests, frustrations, and so on. Sometimes the smallest detail can help your SWC recognize strengths and preferences. As she gets older, you can share your journal entries and verify your observations. Discuss what you both think might be good indicators of future success. You may be amazed at how accurate your evaluations will turn out to be.

My sister is five years younger than I am and, as I've already said, has a considerably more compliant personality. When she was just a toddler, I had already started school. Each day when

I came home, I sat her down in our playroom and taught her what I had learned at school. My mother noticed right away that Sandee had a sharp mind and was a quick study. Mom provided the toys we seemed to want the most: a blackboard, a small school desk, crayons, paper, and books. We played for hours, and Sandee learned to read and do math well before she started kindergarten. In fact, she had been in first grade for just six weeks when the principal suggested she simply skip the rest and start second grade immediately. At the tender ages of seven and two, my sister and I had already shown our parents what would turn out to be vital clues to our future careers. My sister is a successful and happy broker for a real estate and property management company, and I ended up teaching!

Elementary school

When your SWC reaches school age, encourage him to keep a journal or to somehow keep track of his best successes and most frustrating disappointments.

As soon as my sons started school, we began to ask the same two questions every day when they got home: "What did you like about school today?" and "What did you *not* like about school today?" Although many days their answers were predictable (liked recess, didn't like what was served for lunch), we often gained insight into what made them happy and what they were already learning to dread.

If your SWC will keep a journal, suggest she write down the highs and lows of the day or week. If you have a reluctant communicator, try using a dry-erase board or a blackboard and have your SWC complete these two sentences by the end of each day: "The best thing about my day was…" and "The worst thing about my day was…"

The most important goal is to keep the line of communication open between you and your SWC. I encourage you to save the daily or weekly entries and periodically review them with your SWC. It's not only a good reminder of the past, but a strong indicator of what will make your child happy in the future!

The teen years

During the teen years your SWC is likely to have a full schedule, whether it centers on sports, music, or other extracurricular events. Homework, social gatherings, and any number of things will demand your SWC's attention. And yet this is also a time when your teen needs to start seriously thinking about the future and what will happen after high school graduation. You can help your SWC make the most of his experiences and direct his attention to how he can use what happens now to determine his interests and abilities for college and career.

If he's involved in sports, encourage him to identify the aspects of his involvement that are teaching him skills he can use as an adult. If your SWC is participating in music and the arts, help him recognize how the talent he is developing now could turn into part of what makes him successful in finding a vocation he loves.

If your SWC isn't interested in sports or other school activities, one of the best ways to discover talent and passion for a career is to encourage participation in community service. Look for opportunities for your SWC to volunteer his skills and talents in ways that make the world a better place while he tests his interest levels and expertise. Dozens of interesting organizations—such as hospitals, police departments, libraries, nursing homes, and food banks—welcome volunteers while providing on-the-job experience. If you have a hard time motivating your SWC to use some energy productively, try matching the hours he spends volunteering with opportunities to spend the same number of hours doing something he values, like learning to drive the car, having free time, or spending time with friends. The more variety you encourage in the course of doing the volunteer work, the broader your SWC's experiences will be.

How will they find the jobs they love?

Hundreds of books and websites are designed to help both young and old find the perfect career. Interest inventories, seminars, and a multitude of other assessments can help pinpoint appropriate career possibilities. By the time your SWC has reached high school, she should have a good idea of what is most appealing and what is least interesting. The process of a career search need not be complicated or overwhelming, and for the SWC the career choice certainly shouldn't be considered permanent. Often rather than reading pages and pages of job-hunting advice or visiting countless websites, your SWC can receive greater benefit from a direct and simple approach. Here are five realities to keep in mind as you help guide your SWC in the right direction.

1. Don't count on your SWC wanting what you would want.

Each of us is unique. Moreover, your SWC may deliberately choose something different from your preferences just because you seem too pushy or eager. Consciously back off and, whenever possible, limit your suggestions to answering your SWC's questions. Feel free to ask your SWC if he would like your help, but don't take offense if the first answer is no.

2. Chances are good that your SWC will have more than one career.

SWCs are usually very comfortable with the current trend dictating that most people will pursue multiple careers before they retire. Your SWC will almost never settle for staying in one job doing only one thing for the duration of her working years. We

SWCs have little patience for staying in a job we suddenly tire of or that eventually becomes tedious or difficult. Work must seem enjoyable in order for us to stick with it. Similarly, SWCs don't usually hesitate to jump from job to job if necessary. We often believe that anything is better than our present stressful position, and we'll be tempted to bail out without a parachute.

3. Your SWC doesn't mind "jumping through hoops" to get where he needs to be.

Your SWC may be willing to jump through hoops to achieve a goal, but this is true only so long as both you and he recognize they *are* just hoops, not something he's being forced to do. Even the most impatient and carefree SWC might suddenly buckle down and ace chemistry or calculus because that's what it will take to get into the graduate school he wants to attend. But SWCs don't do things just because you and society say we must. We do those things because we're committed to the goals we decide are worth achieving.

4. Your SWC may be prone to go for what looks good at the moment.

Whenever you can help your SWC recognize what a particular job actually entails, it can save a lot of grief. For example maybe your SWC has considered only the more glamorous aspects of being a doctor—the money, the prestige, the life-and-death responsibility. Maybe you, or a friend who is a doctor, could find a gentle way of letting your SWC discover how much training is required, how much detail and work go into the preparation, how much stress and how many potential rules and litigation threats are involved in the day-to-day grind.

Never discourage your SWC from believing he can achieve something through hard work, but do help your SWC decide whether any goal is worth the required sacrifices.

5. Your SWC believes anything is possible.

You may think your arguments about getting good grades ("You need them to get into college") will motivate your SWC to work harder. Most SWCs, however, don't take the threat seriously ("I'll get into college some other way"). Once we actually make up our minds to do something, we'll move heaven and earth to do it. Even if you're convinced we're trying to do the impossible, we love it when you say something like, "It's never been done before, but if anyone can do it, you can."

The bottom line? They've got to try things themselves.

If you're doing your best to help your SWC find and use her strengths and talents, don't get uptight about finding the right niche immediately. By our very nature, we SWCs often must use a trial-and-error approach to make sure we're headed in the right direction. At times we may simply take a time-out and deliberately do something that doesn't further any career. In these instances especially, the more pressure you put on us, the less productive we'll be. If you truly want to help your child find an enjoyable career path, allow her detours and pit stops along the way. Instead of pressuring her to keep moving, do your best to keep emphasizing the most positive aspects of your SWC's nature: determination, tenacity, and resourcefulness.

Chances are good that our SWCs hold the potential to literally change the world. Let's be sure they are headed in the right direction when they do it!

Part III

How to Bring Out the Best in Tough Situations

Every one of these careless words

is going to come back to haunt you.

There will be a time of Reckoning.

Words are powerful; take them seriously.

Words can be your salvation.

Words can also be your damnation.

—Matthew 12:36–37

7

How Can I Survive
a Meltdown?

A Strong-Willed Child Emergency Kit

So, you don't have time to read this whole book right now. But you're on the verge of a meltdown with your strong-willed child, and before everything goes sideways, you need help. Take a deep breath, read these next few pages, and keep an open mind, okay?

For the purpose of this chapter, I'll play the part of the SWC—it's a role I was born to play!

First of all, answer this very important question: Do you have a relationship with this SWC that the child wants to preserve?

If your answer is yes, these strategies should give you almost immediate relief. If your answer is no, these strategies can still be effective, but it will take a little longer to build the trust and rapport you need for long-term results.

Quick reminder: It's not authority strong-willed children have trouble with—it's how the authority is communicated. If you put your finger in my face and tell me I have no choice, you've already lost the battle. I know you can't make me do anything against my free will...except die (figuratively or literally). And I may be willing to do that. I will not let you wrestle my free will away from me. However, if I know you value and respect me, we can build a relationship that can result in my voluntarily submitting to your authority.

Three strategies to regain sanity in the heat of the moment

1. Back off.

If I feel backed into a corner, I probably won't do anything positive about the situation as long as you're making a big issue of it. Once the dust settles and your finger is out of my face, I'll deal with it. By the way, saying it slower and louder isn't going to help. If you're yelling and screaming and threatening, it will only make things worse.

Your SWC is driving you crazy—so do something to get your perspective back in balance. Take a deep breath and say something like, "I'm going to pretend you didn't just say that." Then walk away. Or turn to your SWC and say, "Nice try." Then go on as if you truly believe she didn't mean what she said.

As an SWC, I learned very early in my life how to push your buttons. The only way to reverse this power struggle with your SWC is to keep your voice firm but courteous and respectful. Refuse to be pulled into the argument or baited into losing your cool. Remember, those who anger you, control you.

2. What's the point?

As an SWC, I need rules to make sense to me. I'm much better at aiming my determination in constructive directions when I have compelling problems to solve rather than a list of things to do.

I don't do well with edicts handed down from on high. I want to be a part of the process. I want to at least have some input before final decisions are made. That doesn't mean I have to be in control over you or anyone else. That does mean it brings out the worst in me if I sense you're trying to take away the control I have over myself. If you say things like, "This is the way it's going to be," or, "From now on this is what you're going to do," something inside me wants to rebel and ask, *"You and what army would be making me do that?"*

If you can give me ownership and responsibility and help me find a way to maintain control over my own actions and decisions, you may find me surprisingly cooperative.

For example, most school dress codes are far more easily enforced when students are involved in identifying why a dress code is needed in the first place and in helping set the guidelines for rules and enforcement. Most SWCs will tell you that even if we don't agree with your reasons for the rules, the chances of our cooperation greatly increase when we know you at least *have* some.

Let's look at another example. Let's say you're establishing a weeknight curfew for your teenage daughter. Instead of just telling her what it is, let her know why you're setting one in the first place. In other words, what's the point?

"Sara, we want to make sure you're safe and that you have plenty of time to keep up with your schoolwork during the week. Those two things are pretty important, don't you think?"

Even if she just shrugs or says, "I guess," you have some agreement and you can proceed.

"Knowing you also need a decent amount of sleep, what do you think is fair for a school-night curfew?"

If she says something ridiculous or unacceptable, just calmly keep negotiating.

"Eleven p.m.? Nice try. I was thinking nine."

"What? That's crazy!" she says.

"Okay, let's talk about something in the middle."

You've told her your reasons, asked for her input, and remained firm about a reasonable hour. She has had input, negotiation, and now some ownership in the agreed-upon curfew.

3. Be honest.

Shoot straight with me—don't blow smoke or bluff.

If you're also an SWC (it takes one to know one), here's where it's especially important to think about how *you* would want to be approached. Of course, the downside of being an SWC is that often we can dish it out, but we can't take it. We may find ourselves demanding things of our SWC that *we* wouldn't do. The thing is, we have no reverse gear, and although we probably realized our error the moment we got the words out, we can't undo it.

So just come clean. If you messed up in the way you dealt with me, ask for a do-over. I'll respect you for that and may even go ahead and do what you want me to do.

You're not admitting weakness or surrendering your authority when you're honest with me. You don't ever have to be sorry for holding me to high standards of behavior or achievement. But you may need to actually apologize for the *methods* you insisted I use to accomplish them.

Remember, don't be tentative or indecisive and uncertain when you deal with me. If you seem weak, I have to fight my natural instinct to destroy you. But don't try rolling over me like a steamroller, either. We both know I always have a choice of whether I obey or accept the consequences. So don't pretend that you are the one who has ultimate control over my actions.

The right tools for the job

Given the complications you've faced in the past when dealing with your SWC, you may feel doubtful about how effective this emergency kit will be, but I think you'll be surprised at how easily you can turn things around. Let's recap one more time:

- You need to make sure you have a relationship your SWC wants to preserve.
- If you've backed your SWC into a corner, *back off* and let both of you gain some perspective. Try to make it possible for either or both of you to at least mentally walk away for a bit before you tackle the problem again. This allows both of you to maintain your dignity.
- Ask yourself, *What's the point?* Make sure you have a clear picture of what it is you're trying to accomplish. Then you may actually be able to allow the SWC to get to your bottom line using a different route.
- Be honest with your SWC. I call it my "sliding glass door" theory—we'll see through you anyway, so if you stubbornly insist we can't know what's going on, it will only make things worse. Your honesty and candor will go a long way toward establishing a relationship of trust and cooperation.

Don't hesitate to read this chapter as many times as you need to—then go back and start over at the beginning of the book. And remember, no matter what it seems like right now, the strong-willed child in your life is worth the trouble!

Summing up: Be agreeable, be sympathetic,
be loving, be compassionate, be humble.
That goes for all of you, no exceptions.
No retaliation. No sharp-tongued sarcasm.
Instead, bless—that's your job, to bless.
You'll be a blessing and also get a blessing.

—1 Peter 3:8–9

8

How Do I Keep My Strong-Willed Child from Pulling Our Family Apart?

Strategies for Parents Who Disagree, Blended Families, and Single Parents

I often remind parents what a compliment it is to be trusted with a strong-willed child. Of course, many times it may seem like more of a burden than a gift. This wonderful SWC full of world-changing potential can also drive a wedge into even the most secure and stable family. It's not like it happens on purpose; it just seems to take a lot more time and energy to deal with SWCs than with other, more compliant children. That can create a real problem when you have both kinds of people in your family, but some specific strategies will help you turn conflict into cooperation.

What happens when parents disagree about how to handle the SWC?

After waiting patiently following an evening SWC seminar, a woman hugged me and thanked me for the reassuring advice and encouragement. "But," she said, "I have to tell you I don't know if I can really make a difference with our strong-willed eight-year-old son. I would love to use your strategies, but my husband comes from a strict background, and he's been a police officer for over ten years. He sees Sam's strong will as deliberate defiance of his authority. Won't it only confuse him if I treat him one way and his dad treats him another?"

You may be nodding your head because you're in a similar situation. What if one parent enthusiastically embraces the SWC strategies in this book but the other wants nothing to do with them? There aren't any easy answers to this kind of situation. It's important that both parents agree to and define the outcomes they expect. Accountability can stay intact even when each parent argues about the specific methods used to achieve it. Discuss the situation in private, and preferably in calm and nonconfrontational circumstances. Start by answering the question "What's the point we need to achieve?" and see how many areas of agreement you can find where you both define the same bottom line.

When your SWC plays one parent against the other

Regardless of the parenting situation, SWCs can be notoriously clever at manipulating one parent against another. Although a parent may not consciously play favorites, it's not unusual for a mom or dad to be at odds with a child who won't simply do what she is told to do.

Susan had always been close to her father. An SWC himself, her dad tried to allow Susan some flexibility and options and rarely raised his voice or punished her. Susan's mother was reared in the home of a career military officer, and she thought her husband indulged their daughter too often. After all, Mom believed, rank has its privilege, and children should give their parents unquestioned obedience and learn to follow instructions to the letter. Mom considered her husband's tendency to let Susan have so much decision-making input a weakness. She said she loved her daughter too much to let her stray far from the line. Susan's dad argued he was simply helping their daughter learn to be an independent thinker.

Susan hated doing her homework every evening. Appealing to her dad, she often convinced him the homework could wait until they'd had some fun together. Susan's mom insisted work should always take priority over play. Susan's dad pointed out the work would always be there, but their daughter was growing up quickly. Susan came to see her father as the one who let her do the fun things and her mom as the one who held her back. Her relationship with her mother was strained at best.

By the time Susan was a teenager, the conflict between her parents had reached an unbearable level. On the verge of divorce, the parents turned to a wise marriage-and-family counselor. Susan, of course, needed both parents' perspectives and values. She needed to exhibit good behavior and learn self-discipline. She also needed freedom to make her own decisions and to become responsible and independent. The counselor suggested that Susan's parents work out mutually agreeable ground rules.

Although the exercise was late in coming, they both agreed to make the effort. They often asked each other, "What's the point? What are we trying to accomplish with Susan?" Once they defined their goals—physical safety, personal responsibility, and so on—they were able to hold an after-dinner family conference, share their list of goals with their daughter, and involve her in deciding on some of the methods for achieving them.

Curfew, for example, was a big family issue. Susan hated coming in by ten on the weekends, when most of her friends were staying out until midnight. Mom insisted that she trusted her daughter but wanted her to be safe. Dad argued that she needed to take responsibility for her own decisions. Both parents agreed, however, that Susan's safety was the first priority. Susan and her parents agreed to a midnight curfew on Fridays and Saturdays, with possible exceptions if she called beforehand and informed them where she was and when she would be home. Dad admitted it was necessary to keep track of his daughter's whereabouts, and Mom agreed to trust her daughter's judgment until she had reason not to.

Although it took over a year to see a significant improvement in the relationship between Susan and her mom, the marriage began to recover almost immediately. Over time Susan's mother learned to communicate her love and respect for her daughter by giving her room to negotiate. Susan's dad was able to show his daughter that fun can be a part of accountability, and Susan recognized that although her parents asked her to submit to their authority, they clearly appreciated and respected her.

When you are a single
parent with an SWC

It's crucial for SWCs to feel in control of themselves and their circumstances, so the loss of a parent, whether through death or divorce, can produce insecurity and frustration. As a single parent who is also reeling from a painful situation, consistently showing love and respect for a child who is angry or confused after such a loss may be one of the most difficult tasks you've ever undertaken. If it seems you've lost your ability to stay calm and loving when your SWC has figured out what it takes to make you "lose it," this next illustration may help.

"It's not fair! I hate it here! I'm going to go live with my dad!" If Sally had heard that cry once, she had heard it a hundred times from her ten-year-old son, Ryan. For more than two years, Ryan had held the threat over her head like emotional blackmail. Today, it was different. She was different. Sally took a deep breath and began to put into practice her new parenting approach.

"Ryan, if you go, I'll miss you terribly. But I can't make you stay." She managed to stay calm, which surprised Ryan. He looked at her suspiciously.

"You *want* me to go live with Dad?" he asked.

"No, of course not." Sally smiled and shook her head. "I

want you here with me. But you and I both know the rules around here. If there's just no way you can live with them, and if you're determined to go live with your dad, I won't force you to stay."

Ryan frowned. "But your rules are stupid. Dad never makes me do all this stuff at his house."

Sally nodded empathetically. "I know," she said simply, fighting the urge to make further comment. She stood looking at her son as he watched her face for some sign of anger.

She prayed for strength to hold her ground with Ryan. He knew the words that could make her crazy. He had always been able to push every hot button she had when it came to arguments. But she was determined to hold on to her fragile relationship with him. She had watched it begin to crumble after the divorce and had felt helpless to keep it from breaking apart completely. Ryan was so good at manipulating, so quick to grab opportunities to play his parents against each other. And Sally had been at the end of her rope with so many things at once—the divorce, the stress of her job, the guilt about what the whole situation was doing to Ryan. She had found herself yelling at him for almost everything. But she knew more now. She was not about to let her son slip away.

Ryan was waiting for her to react in her usual way, and he

was uncertain what to do when she didn't yell at him. His resolve seemed to be melting. Sally reached over to give him a quick hug.

"Ryan, do you know what I like about you?" she asked. When he shook his head, her heart almost broke. Was it possible he didn't know how much she loved him?

"Sweetheart, I like how you help keep this house together when I feel that everything's falling apart. I like how you watch my favorite old TV show with me every night before bed and then let me tuck you in. And I especially like how you stand up for what you believe, even when others may not agree with you. Ryan, you are a wonderful kid, and I'm so lucky to have you."

Ryan tried not to smile, but he didn't resist her hug. "Does that mean I don't have to take the trash out after all?" he asked. Sally gave him a playful shove.

"Nice try," she told him. "How about I help you and we'll get it done twice as fast?"

He shrugged and nodded. "I need to call Dad," he said. Sally's heart almost stopped. Ryan nodded again. "I think I'd better tell him I won't be seeing him until this weekend after all."

Being a single parent presents an incredible and exhausting challenge, even when you have a compliant child. Put an SWC into the mix, and it can be a recipe for disaster! But a couple of practical solutions can bring quick relief.

- *Try "trading" SWCs with another single parent for a day.* Often a change of perspective can give you a little breathing room. Also, sometimes dealing with a different SWC can help you be more objective with your own. When you trade back, be sure you and the other parent share some of the things you liked best about the other's SWC. Start out with something similar to this: "One of the things I like most about Josh is…"

- *Ask a parent you admire to be your mentor— preferably someone who has succeeded in raising an SWC of his own.* Find someone who would welcome occasional phone calls and give sensitive, nonjudgmental advice. You'll want to make it easy for your prospective mentor—don't ask for lengthy answers or request time out of a too-busy schedule. Tell him what you propose to do in a particular situation, and get feedback and suggestions. Don't feel self-conscious about asking for help when you're overwhelmed. Most good mentors will be honored that you've asked for their advice.

When you have a blended
family and an SWC

It's especially challenging to deal with an SWC in a blended family. Not only do you have the task of adjusting to a new spouse, but you also have to accept and accommodate children with complex and mysterious learning styles and personality traits that were not in any way inherited from you.

I've spoken to dozens of moms and dads who are struggling to love and understand an SWC who seems determined to undermine the new family structure. One frustrated mother admitted she had reached the point with her twelve-year-old SWC stepson where she simply no longer wanted to spend the energy trying to love him. "I take care of his physical needs," she assured me, "but I just won't let him jerk my emotions around anymore. He thinks I hate him, and I'm so tired of going head to head with him every day that I think I'll just let him see that I'm withdrawing from the whole relationship."

I understood her frustration. She's an SWC herself, and her almost-teenaged stepson had figured out the quickest way to drive her into a corner nearly every time they spoke to each other. He knew how to pit his father against his stepmother, and he used his biological mother as another piece of ammunition. He got by with a lot of bad behavior, and his stepmother felt powerless to enforce the rules without her husband's full support.

This situation is all too familiar. Discipline and account-ability, of course, must stay intact. At no time do I advocate letting the SWC get by with bad behavior. But before any dis-cipline strategies can have the desired effect, a positive relation-ship must be established between all parties involved. I've dealt with many parents who have reached the end of their ropes with their biological children. It's no wonder that parents struggle when they have to learn to love another person's dif-ficult child. But you simply can't have a healthy family without building and sustaining a loving and respectful relationship with each child. Of course, each child needs to respect his par-ents as well, but since we're the grownups, we need to set the example.

When a parent gives up and decides to withdraw from the relationship with a child, devastating results almost always fol-low: attention-getting misbehavior, self-medication through illegal drugs, seeking to find approval elsewhere. Although it may be difficult to keep the relationship positive, when there's no relationship at all, parents lose any leverage or motivation that might have worked. A family can't survive without uncon-ditional love for one another. That doesn't mean you must ac-cept whatever behavior your child decides to give you. Instead, it means you maintain a firm but loving attitude even when you have to enforce rules and consequences, such as loss of phone privileges, reduction in allowance, or missing an important social event.

An SWC knows you can't force him to love or accept you. He also knows he doesn't have to do what you say. The one thing he doesn't know is whether or not you'll go on loving him no matter what. After all, he's already lost at least one parent. What assurance does he have that you'll stick around for him? It won't be easy, but you can help him develop confidence in you and in his new family situation.

Look for ways you can show him how serious you are about your commitment to the blended family. Even small gestures, such as the following, can mean a lot to an SWC who is looking for signs of security.

- *Suggest putting together a time capsule.* Ask all the members of the family to contribute items that will always remind them of this turning point in their lives. Encourage each one to write at least a brief note about how he or she is feeling, then seal the notes and the items in an envelope. Decide together what date in the future you will open the time capsule.

- *Look for opportunities to talk about your future as a new family.* For example, buy tickets for a show that's months in the future, or post a calendar that tracks a full year's activities.

• *When your SWC (or any of your children) witnesses an argument between you and your new spouse, take time to reassure him the relationship is still strong and loving.* No matter how difficult the adjustments are, your children need to know your commitment will stay intact. Your respect for each child's unique contributions to the family will build and cement the lifelong relationship.

Be prepared. You're up against far more
than you can handle on your own.
Take all the help you can get, every weapon
God has issued, so that when it's all over
but the shouting you'll still be on your feet.
Truth, righteousness, peace, faith, and salvation
are more than words. Learn how to apply them.
You'll need them throughout your life.
God's Word is an indispensable weapon.
In the same way, prayer is essential
in this ongoing warfare. Pray hard and long.
Pray for your brothers and sisters.
Keep your eyes open. Keep each other's spirits up
so that no one falls behind or drops out.

—Ephesians 6:13–18

9

When Should I Do Something Drastic?

Recognizing Signs of Serious Trouble

The telephone rang at 3:02 a.m., according to the digital clock radio. Charles was barely awake as he reached for the phone, but his wife, Jennifer, was instantly alert. "It's got to be about Angie," she said quietly. Her heart beat wildly in her chest. Their seventeen-year-old SWC had missed her curfew again. Somehow, Jennifer knew this transgression would have more serious consequences than others in the past. Her husband listened intently to the voice on the telephone.

As he hung up, Jennifer was already on her feet. Sitting on the side of the bed, Charles put his head in his hands. He spoke slowly. "Angie was driving. She and Gina and Roger left a wild party, started home by way of Parker Road, and took the corner too fast. The car rolled over several times and hit a tree." Seeing the panic on Jennifer's face, Charles continued quickly. "Angie's going to be all right. She was wearing a seat belt and just has a broken arm and some bruises. Roger is in serious condition." He paused. "Gina didn't make it."

The phone call changed their family's life forever. Jennifer and Charles had struggled with Angie's strong-willed nature for years, but during the past twenty-four months their relationship had deteriorated. Angie had made some poor choices in friends, and her schoolwork hit the skids almost immediately. When her parents insisted she improve her grades and control her social life, Angie reacted with extreme rebellion and explosive anger.

Jennifer had sensed their loss of parental control months ago but felt helpless to reverse the situation. Charles had just wanted the problem to go away and hoped this was a phase their daughter would grow out of. But Angie's behavior had continued to spiral downward. She shoplifted small items from a corner grocery store. She lied to her mother. She cheated on a test at school and threatened another student. She hung around at parties where there was a lot of underage drinking. And recently Jennifer had begun to suspect that Angie was experimenting with drugs. Appointments with school counselors, church pastors, and teen-group leaders had all failed to produce any positive results.

And then came the early-morning phone call.

Gina had been Angie's best friend since grade school. When

the hospital tested Angie for drugs and alcohol right after the accident, the results showed she was under the influence of both. She was not only in trouble with the law, but she was also responsible for the death of the one person she felt understood her. Depression set in swiftly and intensely. Two weeks after the accident, Angie attempted suicide.

Her parents were frantic and, on the advice of a hospital psychologist, had their unwilling daughter committed to a youth rehabilitation center. The center's program was rigorous and unyielding, and Angie's strong will presented a tremendous obstacle to her success there. After she almost succeeded in her second suicide attempt, Angie and her parents met with a highly recommended counselor who specialized in dealing with SWCs. The four of them carefully explored the options and then chose another program that seemed to be more compatible with Angie's style and temperament. Although the road will be long and the journey arduous, Angie and her parents are on the upward trail.

Angie's story is not unusual, especially for SWCs. Perhaps you have had a similar experience or know someone who has been through a devastating crisis with a child. As a result of talking to and working with families like Angie's over the past several years, I have discovered some definite patterns as well as some tried and true strategies for dealing with an SWC who has gone too far. I am not a counselor, and I am certainly not an expert on psychological or criminal behaviors. But there are some general guidelines that can help you choose the right professionals and recognize when you need them most.

When has strong-willed behavior gone too far?

This is a good time to remind you that strong will is not, by itself, a negative trait. Angie's problem is not her strong will—it's how she used it and what direction it took. And she's going to need that strong will more than ever to succeed in her rehabilitation.

Hopefully you have already benefited from the suggestions in this book so far, and your relationship with your strong-willed child is destined to just keep getting better. There's no question it won't be easy, and you'll probably experience a lot of frustration along with your successes in working with your SWC.

But there are times when, difficult as it may be, parents must face the realization that their SWC has crossed a line, and the situation is spiraling out of control. At that point, no amount of discipline or creative motivation strategies can turn the tide. It calls for professional intervention and help to prevent your SWC from harming himself or others.

I was conducting a parenting seminar for a small group of frustrated parents of SWCs. During the question and discussion period, one mother raised her hand. "If I don't do what she wants, my four-year-old strong-willed daughter tells me she's going to run out in the street and let a car run over her." As the audience gasped, I quickly told this distressed mom she needed to take immediate action to get a professional counselor or therapist involved. This is not simply an issue of strong will.

A few months later, a woman came up to talk with me after an SWC seminar. If tears hadn't been streaming down her face, I would have thought she was kidding when she said, "I can't believe I'm telling you this, but I have a horrible strong-willed son who's six years old. It's getting so awful that I've been thinking lately it wouldn't be so bad if he got kidnapped—as long as he wasn't tortured." Here is a family who needs more than a book full of insights and strategies. They need professional help and support.

So how do you decide the time has come when you can no longer handle your SWC on your own? There are no simple answers, but here are some questions that can help you examine specific areas of life with your SWC and determine whether things have gone too far:

- *Physical safety:* Is your SWC's life in danger? Is your SWC endangering the lives of others?
- *Moral and spiritual values:* Is your SWC deliberately disregarding longstanding household rules or violating your and your family's basic moral values?

- *Destructive behavior:* Is your SWC causing property damage or harming people's possessions, including his own?
- *Dishonesty:* Have you caught your SWC deliberately lying or hiding the truth?

If you answered yes to any of the above questions, you should be concerned. If you realize you've lost control over any of these areas, it's time for you to reach out and take action to get help from trusted professionals.

What to do if you've lost control

If you feel you have lost control over your SWC, it's important to take the following seven decisive steps as quickly as possible.

1. Pray and discuss.

Talk to your spouse or those who support you emotionally. Take an honest look at whether you've lost the ability to control your child. Identify the point at which you lost influence over your SWC. Rededicate your child to God—and commit your desires and efforts to finding and doing what's best for your child.

2. Deal with the issues in front of you.

Try to make your decisions based on what's happening right now. Don't blame others or take on a lot of guilt for past events that led to the current situation. Everyone will certainly share the responsibility. Also, many factors are simply not under your control. Every SWC has a free will, and you can only do so much to influence his life choices. Just because you need to call upon professional help doesn't mean you're a failure as a parent. At this point, it will be counterproductive to try to place blame or to spend your energy criticizing or scolding yourself or others.

3. Decide what you need to accomplish.

The severity of the action you take with your SWC will depend on the nature of your crisis. Although you don't want to over-react, neither do you want to underestimate the seriousness of a potential emotional or substance-abuse problem.

- Do you need to separate your SWC from the rest of the family to ensure anyone's physical safety?
- Is it likely that your child could attempt suicide?
- Does your child simply need time and space for a cooling-off period?
- Would it help if the family communicated better?

Decide what your objectives should be for getting help with your SWC. Ideally, you should sit down with the family and make a list of what you feel you need to accomplish. Even if you are dealing with an immediate, heat-of-the-moment crisis, take the time to ask that important question: What's the point?

What are we trying to accomplish here? If you don't know what you want to accomplish, how will you know whether you have been successful?

4. Find the right professionals.

There are effective programs, counselors, and medical/mental-health professionals throughout the nation and the world. But even the most thoroughly professional program with documented success can be counterproductive if it employs techniques that are opposed to your SWC's nature and mind-set. Knowing this doesn't necessarily mean you'll be able to find a program that your SWC will like, but it does mean you'll increase your chances of finding one that actually works over the long haul.

Be sure your professional has documentation of state licenses, memberships in national professional associations, solid credentials, and specific expertise. Beyond that, you can ask some important questions to help determine whether this person or organization will be a good match and work well with your child.

- What is the mission and goal of the organization?
- How will you control the behavior of my child?
- How will we know we've chosen the right program?
- Do you try to break the spirit or simply control the will? How will you do that?

- What kind of training does the staff have that specifically addresses the needs and issues of an SWC?
- At what point would we decide the program has accomplished its goals?

5. Seek several opinions.

Don't just grab the first solution that presents itself. Seek the advice of those you trust most, especially friends or acquaintances who have successfully reared their own SWCs. You will probably get more opinions than you want, and the strongest ones may come from parents who don't have any idea what you're experiencing. Try to keep your perspective and do your best not to let others determine how you feel. Ask more than one health professional about your situation, and press for specialists if you feel it's necessary. Trust your instincts as a parent. Although you don't want to become unreasonable or obsessive, you may have to be assertive with your requests for attention.

Remember, each of these steps will take time. As much as you want to seek immediate relief from a miserable situation, the recovery period for your child may take weeks, months, or even years. Look for and celebrate small victories. Keep your expectations realistic, and stay open to the possibility that you'll need to start over once or twice in order to find the right approach. Don't give up!

6. Don't try to do this by yourself.

Find other parents and family members who understand. Spend your time with those who won't simply criticize. Do the best you can, and resist the urge to second-guess yourself.

7. Love your SWC, and communicate that love as often as possible.

Don't waver in your resolve to find the best way to keep your SWC safe and healthy without sacrificing other family members or other people.

Hang on to hope.

I've never met a parent who wasn't willing to spend any amount of time or money if it meant her child would be saved. I've seen dozens of parents who have mortgaged everything they own and spent years paying back debts and starting over in new careers just so they could find a way for their SWCs to be safe, productive, and successful.

You may be reading this right now through a haze of pain and sorrow because of what your SWC is doing. While there are no guarantees, there is hope. The steps you take may be unpleasant, expensive, and time-consuming, but your child is worth it. God did not give you this child by accident. Trust

Him and accept the compliment you've been given. There's help when you've reached the end of your rope. You don't have to go through this alone. This may be the hardest thing you'll ever do, but it could most certainly be the most worthwhile.

God's servant must not be argumentative,

but a gentle listener and a teacher who keeps cool,

working firmly but patiently with those

who refuse to obey. You never know how

or when God might sober them up with a change

of heart and a turning to the truth.

—2 Timothy 2:24–25

10

Is It Too Late to Restore a Relationship with My Strong-Willed Child?

Insights for Reaching an SWC Who Doesn't Want to Be Reached

A woman in her late fifties approached me after one of my SWC seminars. "I did everything wrong," she sobbed. "I did and said all those things to my daughter that you just told us won't work." She took a deep breath and began to explain how she had tried to bully her daughter into submission, frequently using threats and severe punishment. "My daughter is grown now," she said sadly, "and she's working as an attorney in California. She returns all of my letters unopened and refuses to communicate with me in any way. How can I ever tell her how sorry I am?"

Unfortunately, this mother's plight mirrors that of dozens

of other parents I've spoken to over the years. So many tell me essentially the same thing:

"Where were you twenty years ago?"

"It's too late now—my strong-willed child is grown."

"Why didn't I know this when I could still do something about it?"

It's never too late to say you're sorry.

The fact is, you *can* do something about it. As long as both you and your SWC are living, it's not too late to begin the process of healing your relationship. For this particular mother, the solution turned out to be simple and straightforward. She mailed a copy of *You Can't Make Me* to her daughter with a brief, boldly lettered note on the envelope that read, "Here's what I did wrong—I'm sorry."

She and I agreed there was a good chance her SWC attorney daughter would find it hard to resist the urge to at least take a look at what her mother claimed was an admission of guilt. Once the ice was broken, perhaps they could both talk about the past in less personal terms. I also reminded this mother that she did not have to apologize for the outcomes she had desired—self-discipline, good manners, personal responsibility. Instead, she was apologizing for demanding exactly *how* those outcomes were achieved.

Parents of teenage SWCs are often troubled when they realize how different things could have been if they had known more about how the SWC's mind works early in the relationship. In their book *Parenting with Love and Logic,* Foster Cline and Jim Fay give discouraged parents some reassurance:

> It usually takes one month of love-and-logic parenting
> to undo one year of tacky parenting. So, if your child
> is twelve years old, give yourself twelve months to help
> her learn responsible thinking.... It's never too late....
> The important thing is to build a relationship with our
> kids that will last a lifetime—long past the end of the
> teenage years. And it is never too late to work on that.[1]

I love getting success letters from parents who have embraced this truth in their families. It's not easy, and they often make several starts and stops before seeing noticeable progress. But the rewards are incredibly satisfying, and the reclaimed relationship with a son or daughter can last a lifetime. Gwen Ellis, my first and favorite professional book editor, wrote a letter to me:

> My son and I are very much alike—like a pair of old
> shoes. There are lots and lots of things we don't need
> to talk about. We just know what the other is thinking.

That makes it easy for us to be together, have serious discussions, and understand how the other learns.

My daughter and I are very different, and I drive her crazy. I grasp things quickly and am ready to move on to the next thing. She's still back there gathering more and more information before she's ready to move on. You can see how difficult it is for us to communicate. When I began to understand aspects of SWCs and the different learning styles, I began to share what I was reading with her. She began reading your material and learning with me—and what a difference it has made.

We knew we were making progress when the two of us went to a home and garden show. When we came in the door, she stopped me and said, "Mom, I can't stand the way you do these shows. You go here and there and all over the place. How do you know when you've seen everything?" In my mind I thought, *Who cares if you see everything?* I bit my lip because she obviously did care.

"Okay. How do you want to do this?" I asked.

"Let's go around to each booth in a circle."

"All right, but do you have to read every word of every sign?"

"No," she said and grinned.

We proceeded in an orderly fashion around the

room and saw what we wanted to see and had an absolutely great time together.

Coming to understand our differences has probably saved our relationship. It taught us that we weren't trying to make each other miserable. We really love each other. What was wrong between us was more about the way we receive and process information than it was about mother-daughter warfare.

My daughter was in her late twenties when we discovered this, and we had been in confrontation for years. But when we both began to learn about each other, we were able to move forward in our relationship and understand we will never approach life in the same way—and that's all right.

There *is* hope, no matter how long it has been since you and your SWC have had a positive relationship. You won't find easy answers or quick fixes, but genuine, loving, sustained efforts can bring about more changes than you ever thought possible. Frankly, I believe that dealing with an SWC often takes supernatural strength and wisdom. When we try to transform a relationship on our own, we frequently fail. Certainly in my own experience as an SWC, and as the parent of one, a strong faith in God has made all the difference.

Help! I think I've blown it!

If you feel that you've blown it with your SWC, don't give up. I've collected a few tips from my prodigal SWC friends to give you some ideas for bringing your child back. Here are six of them:

1. Start leaving notes.

Point out what you like and appreciate about your child. Thank your SWC for something; give praise for a good idea. Even a quick sticky note on a bedroom door can speak volumes. If your SWC has left home, a quick text message, an electronic greeting card, or even a small gift can work wonders.

2. Apologize for insisting on always doing things your way.

Explain the outcomes you were trying to achieve and let your SWC know you are open to other suggestions for achieving the same goal.

3. Don't let your SWC scare you away or make you angry.

Hang in there! Let your child rant and rave if she must, but remain unmoved when it comes to offering your love. She may tell you there's no hope, she may claim she hates you, she may insist all is lost—but don't believe it! Your SWC just has to make sure you won't actually give up on her.

4. Be consistent.

We SWCs will watch for a chink in your armor. We'll be suspicious that your new attitude won't last. Try to enlist the help of another family member and identify a code word or phrase. When you're talking to your SWC and that family member realizes things are beginning to go downhill, she can say the code phrase and alert you to what's happening.

5. Find a way to reconnect.

If your SWC has left home, try reestablishing contact by sending a copy of this book with a note similar to the one sent by the mother mentioned at the opening of this chapter. By pointing out that the contents may explain what you did wrong, two things could happen: first, your SWC may be intrigued enough to read it; and second, your SWC may realize what he did wrong as well.

6. Pray.

Many SWCs have told me they were compelled by God to return home, certain the prayers of their family brought them back. While your SWC is at home, pray together whenever possible. Let your child hear you talking to God about your relationship, especially when you're thanking Him for giving you such a great kid. Be specific with God regarding what you love about your SWC. Those prayers can also help remind you what you like about your child when the stress level is high!

Qualities every parent can possess

People often ask me how my parents figured out what to do with me as I was growing up. How did they know what strategies would work for such a strong-willed child before there were any books about it? Sometimes I overhear my mom or dad as they answer the questions asked directly to them. They both smile and claim it wasn't as hard as you think. After all, God is good and wise and merciful, and He has always been at the center of their marriage, directing their family.

My parents both came from extremely dysfunctional families. My dad—from whom I inherited my strong will, by the way—grew up the son of a wealthy business owner who divorced the mother of his children to marry his secretary. My father and his brother were reared primarily by their mother, who ran a tavern and had many pursuits besides parenting. The two boys learned street smarts right away, and both of them quickly adopted the credo "Only the strong survive."

Dad started drinking at a young age, and his cigarette habit started just as early. Because he and his brother had a great deal of talent, they made a living by playing honky-tonk piano at bars and nightclubs. Their act was "Four Hands on One Piano," and the female clientele especially loved the two handsome men who seemed just as accomplished in wine and women as they were in song.

Dad joined the U.S. Navy and served in World War II and in the Korean War. He came close to death more than once, and one night, during a drunken stupor in an alley behind a tavern, he stood alone and looked up to the heavens. He was miserable and lonely and fed up with his life. For the first time ever, he prayed, "God, if you're really out there, help me."

Stateside, he rented a tiny room from an elderly lady in Wichita, Kansas. Mrs. Poslick had no formal experience in dealing with strong-willed, rebellious, and wild-living young men. But she did have an extremely strong faith in God, and somehow she knew He wanted this young man to do something special with his life. My dad stayed out late every Saturday night, drinking and partying. Although his Sunday-morning hangovers were acute, Mrs. Poslick's bacon-and-eggs cooking always lured him out of bed. Bleary-eyed and sheepish, he would sit at the breakfast table with this godly woman, and she would feed him until he was full. She didn't flinch when he let the swear words slip out. She didn't lecture him about the strong odors of liquor and cigarettes.

"Bob," she would say pleasantly as he finished eating, "would you like to go to Sunday school with me?" He always groaned to himself. She had been so nice, given him so much.

How could he refuse her? Reluctantly, he began to attend church, and God got hold of his life so firmly that a few weeks later he surrendered his heart and his strong will to Christ.

Over the course of the next few months, he decided on his own to quit drinking, smoking, and swearing. He frequently tells the story of how those wonderful church folks never pressured him to give up his vices. He admits he shocked a few of the elderly ladies at first with his language when he testified in church. But they loved him and prayed for him and brought him casseroles and pastries. Not wanting to disappoint them, he cleaned up his act and figured out what was pleasing to his Lord and Savior. It wasn't long before he knew in his heart that God had called him to be a full-time minister of the gospel that had rescued him in the first place. He accepted the call, used his GI bill to enter a Christian college, and broke the news to his father.

My grandfather had been counting on my dad and his brother to take over the family business, so when my dad shared his new faith and calling, my grandfather exploded. Didn't he understand what he was giving up? He was set to make a fortune! This whole Christianity thing was ridiculous! My grandfather said he would take no part in Dad's life if he chose to pursue it. With deep sadness, my dad left, praying that somehow God would change his father's heart. Dad enrolled in college and embraced a new life that would eventually include a woman he'd meet there.

My grandfather took quick and decisive action by disowning my father and ostracizing him from the family. Dad spent over forty years praying for his father, despite many people telling him it wasn't working. His strong will wouldn't let him give up. The two men were reconciled several years later, but it wasn't until a few months before my grandfather died that Dad was given the ultimate gift of leading his strong-willed father to the Lord.

My mom had already finished her college degree when my dad showed up on campus. She worked in the dean's office, and with the help of her boss's matchmaking skills, she met and married my dad. Mom had come from a pretty dysfunctional family herself. Her biological mother died giving birth to her, and she was separated from her father and six siblings. She had been adopted by her mother's sister, who raised her in a home where she was welcome but lived uneasily. Her uncle was mentally ill and verbally abusive. She and her aunt both lived in fear of him, and by the time he died (well after my mother had left home), he had inflicted fear and intimidation on both of them.

Despite her upbringing, my mom developed a firm faith in God, and she was determined to make a success of her life. She graduated from college with honors and set a course for a career in business or education. When she married my dad, she was undaunted by his enthusiasm and strong will. Together they began a home mission church in a small town in Missouri, and over the next fifty years, their ministry touched thousands of lives.

My dad was an adult before he ever gained control of his strong will. There are those who would have said that he seemed, in many ways, beyond redemption. It had gone so far, he had done so much—how could any good come out of this? But one godly woman started praying for him and loving him and winning him through her unwavering faith in a God who created the very will that Dad used against Him. Was it too late? Absolutely not! My dad stands as living proof that an errant, strong-willed individual can be redeemed and used for the kingdom of God. My parents reared my sister and me in a home that bore no resemblance to the dysfunctional ones they came from. We were grounded in faith, dedicated to service, and educated in the ways of both heaven and the world.

When I asked my dad to write a paragraph or two from his point of view for this chapter, he penned the following note to me:

You knew that your mom and I loved each other deeply, and that you never had to worry about our commitment to Jesus and to each other. Remember the story you told about us holding hands under the breakfast table? We are still doing it.

We never brought home the personal problems of those we ministered to. No matter what anyone did, Mom and I never became bitter or negative, and we were never any different at home than we were in public.

It was in Reno that we decided there was power in positive thinking, and challenged you and Sandee to look at life in a positive rather than in a negative way. Remember it cost us a nickel a negative word? That didn't last long, because we couldn't afford it!

You have stated the facts clearly and concisely in a beautiful way. You are still directing a strong will sanctified by Jesus in a loving, generous, positive way. Thank you for making your mother and me a great part of your life—even up to this very minute.

It's true my parents had no formal training in raising a spirited and strong-willed child like me. But they did have two things that every parent can possess: a life wholly and firmly committed to God and an unconditional love for their strong-willed child.

In the end, these qualities are what really matter.

Never give up!

Sadly, I've talked to a number of parents who say they have lost the drive and energy it takes to start over and restore a good relationship with their SWC. What can you do if you have lost the will to go on? What if the whole situation simply seems too overwhelming? I don't believe parents of SWCs can cultivate and maintain these often fragile relationships purely through our own efforts.

Over the many years that I've been an SWC, have parented an SWC, and have worked with other parents of SWCs, I have seen only one effective solution for rebuilding and recovering relationships that are so far gone: God, who created us in the first place, can restore love and renew the desire to keep our relationships strong and healthy. On our own, we humans simply don't have the resources or energy to deal with the daily challenges of life with an SWC.

If you feel that you have exhausted your options—if you have had it—and you don't see any way to rebuild your relationship with your SWC, let me offer you the best hope I have found, bar none. *Trust the wisdom of the God who created your SWC in the first place. Pray for guidance and wisdom and, most of all, the desire to love your child unconditionally.* It takes more strength than you have, but God has an abundant store of mercy and grace, and it's when we reach the end of our own resources that He can do His best. Don't despair if things don't change immediately. Keep praying, and keep working on your attitude.

Don't give up—with God's help you can do more than you think!

Get along among yourselves, each of you
doing your part. Our counsel is that you warn
the freeloaders to get a move on.
Gently encourage the stragglers, and reach out
for the exhausted, pulling them to their feet.
Be patient with each person, attentive
to individual needs. And be careful that when
you get on each other's nerves you don't snap
at each other. Look for the best in each other,
and always do your best to bring it out.

—1 Thessalonians 5:14–15

Epilogue
Start Right Where You Are

After teaching a seminar that's particularly intense and full of substance, I like to leave my audience with some comforting words. I'd like to do the same for you.

You've made it to the end of this book, and your head is filled with thoughts, ideas, questions, and eager anticipation for trying some of these strategies with your own strong-willed child. But you may also find yourself a little overwhelmed, wondering which ones will work and where to start. Believe it or not, that's where I want you to be by the time you reach this point. I'd much rather have you feel a little confused and uncertain than for you to be so confident that you use the tools like just another set of formulas. That can make you armed and dangerous rather than informed and adventurous. The strategies we've discussed here are meant not as instructions to be rigidly followed but as creativity boosters for your ongoing efforts to understand, appreciate, and communicate with the SWC in your life.

There's no magic formula for achieving a strong relationship with your child. You don't have to be a perfect parent.

Remember how much confidence God has in you since He gave you this SWC. You can be successful in restoring and maintaining a positive relationship with that SWC in ways you may never have thought about before. You can be one of the most powerful influencers in your SWC's life and you can celebrate the ways the world will be a better place because your SWC is in it.

One more thing: most of the strategies in this book come with an expiration date (but not one you can see ahead of time). They work well for a while, then they seem to lose their initial effectiveness. Don't worry—that's totally normal. Just put that strategy on the shelf for a season and use another one. Don't give up on the former strategy, though. After a period of time it will work again, and a different strategy will take a break for a while.

Also, I encourage you to resist the temptation to tackle every issue at once when it comes to dealing with your SWC. On the next page you'll find a list of Top Ten Tips that bring out the best in just about any SWC. This list can be a powerful resource for you, but it would be overwhelming for you and your SWC if you tried to tackle everything on the list at once. Pick one at a time and try it. Don't give up too easily—it may take your SWC a little time to believe you are serious about changing the relationship.

This is only the beginning! You're about to discover how enjoyable and rewarding it can be to live with an SWC!

Top Ten Tips for Bringing Out the Best in an SWC of Any Age

1. Value my ability to see the world from a unique perspective.
   Find ways to appreciate and make the most of my strengths, even when I annoy you.

2. Remember, we need compelling problems to solve, not just chores to do.
   Don't be the "big boss." I'll respect your authority more when you tell me the point.

3. Ask for my input; keep me in the information loop.
   Give me some ownership in the process and the outcome.

4. Protect our relationship—you won't get much from me without one.
   Respect and value who I am, and I'll cooperate with you most of the time.

5. Smile at me more often.
   Keep your sense of humor and try to smile, even when you don't like me.

6. Don't let me push you around, but don't push me around either.

    Don't be afraid to stand up to me; just don't run over me.

7. Speak to me respectfully, but firmly.

    Use your voice wisely; it's a powerful resource.

8. Choose your battles—don't sweat the small stuff.

    Decide what's really worth it.

9. Give me some control over my own life and circumstances.

    Allow me to share control without surrendering your authority.

10. Remind me how much you love me.

    Find subtle ways to keep reminding me your love will always be there.

A Last Word

If you've benefited from this book, I'd love to hear from you. Perhaps you have a success story that would help others. Maybe you have unanswered questions I could address in a future book. Please drop me a line, and I'll do my best to address your issues and concerns. You can contact me at:

Apple St., LLC (Applied Learning Styles)
P.O. Box 23162
Federal Way, WA 98093
www.AppleSt.com
ctapplest@gmail.com

Acknowledgments

I'd like to gratefully acknowledge just a few of those who helped make this book a reality:

Thank you to my strong-willed and loving husband, Jack, who is the perfect partner for this strong-willed woman.

Thank you also to my dad and mom, Robert and Minnie Ulrich, who have been shining examples of a strong marriage (sixty years at this writing) and wise and godly parenting.

My boys, Mike and Robert, have taught me how to truly appreciate strong will at its best, and both of them have also given me countless opportunities to learn patience and practice the strategies in this book.

A huge thank you to my wonderful editor, Gwen Ellis. She's been with me through thick and thin, and no one knows how to motivate me as an author better than she does.

I would especially like to thank the hundreds of strong-willed children and adults of all ages who continue to share their stories and insights with me.

To God be the glory!

Notes

Chapter 4: What About the Line Between Right and Wrong?

1. Steve Green, "Find Us Faithful," words and music by Jon Mohr. Copyright © 1987 Jonathan Mark Music and Birdwing Music. All rights controlled by Gaither Copyright Management. Used by permission.

Chapter 5: So What's the Big Deal About School?

1. Sharon Begley, "Where Do Great Minds Come From? And Why Are There No Einsteins, Freuds or Picassos Today?" *Newsweek*, June 28, 1993, 46–50.

2. Peter R. Breggin and Ginger Ross Breggin, *The War Against Children: How the Drugs, Programs, and Theories of the Psychiatric Establishment Are Threatening America's Children with a Medical "Cure" for Violence* (New York: St. Martin's, 1994), 110.

3. Robert J. Martin, *Teaching Through Encouragement: Techniques to Help Students Learn* (Englewood Cliffs, NJ: Prentice-Hall, 1980), 7.

Chapter 10: Is It Too Late to Restore a Relationship with My Strong-Willed Child?

1. Foster Cline and Jim Fay, *Parenting with Love and Logic* (Colorado Springs, CO: NavPress, 2006), 61.

Recommended Resources

Armstrong, Thomas. *The Myth of the A.D.D. Child: 50 Ways to Improve Your Child's Behavior and Attention Span Without Drugs, Labels, or Coercion.* New York: Dutton Books, 1995. A former special-education teacher, Dr. Armstrong provides fifty practical, positive ways to help that child who has been labeled with A.D.D. (attention deficit disorder). His heartfelt and well-researched position is that A.D.D. does not exist; the children who experience behavioral and attention-related problems are healthy human beings with a unique style of thinking and learning.

Breggin, Peter R., and Ginger Ross Breggin. *The War Against Children: How the Drugs, Programs, and Theories of the Psychiatric Establishment Are Threatening America's Children with a Medical "Cure" for Violence.* New York: St. Martin's, 1994. Dr. Peter Breggin is a psychiatrist who has taken a stand against the use of medication for social control of children and their behaviors. He and his wife have written this compelling book, providing a host of alternative measures for fulfilling the genuine and often inconvenient needs of children.

Chess, Stella, and Alexander Thomas. *Know Your Child: An Authoritarian Guide for Today's Parents.* New York: Basic

Books, 1987. This volume is packed with evidence (including longitudinal research studies) that each child has his own unique temperament from the beginning to the end of his life. Their "goodness of fit" theory has practical applications for successful parenting.

Cline, Foster, and Jim Fay. *Parenting Teens with Love and Logic: Preparing Adolescents for Responsible Adulthood.* Colorado Springs: Piñon, 1993. Whether you've used the love-and-logic approach all along or are looking for some extra help during adolescence, this book will give you a fresh look at discipline, self-esteem, and common struggles parents have with their teenagers. You win because you'll learn to love and effectively guide your teens without resorting to anger, threats, or power struggles. Your teens win because they'll learn responsibility and problem solving with the tools they'll need to cope in the real world.

Cline, Foster, and Jim Fay. *Parenting with Love and Logic: Teaching Children Responsibility.* Colorado Springs: Piñon, 1990. If you want to raise kids who are self-confident, motivated, and ready for the real world, take advantage of this win-win approach to parenting. The information in this book will not only revolutionize your relationships with your children, but it might also put the fun back into parenting!

Glenn, H. Stephen, and Jane Nelsen. *Raising Self-Reliant Children in a Self-Indulgent World: Seven Building Blocks for Developing Capable Young People.* Rocklin, CA: Prima, 1989. A wonderful, practical, and real-world handbook for helping even strong-willed children learn to be independent without getting away with bad behavior. You'll love the evenhanded, down-to-earth approach taken by these two authors, one a parent of seven, the other a parent of four and foster parent of twenty.

Keirsey, David, and Marilyn Bates. *Please Understand Me: Character and Temperament Types.* Del Mar, CA: Prometheus Nemesis, 1978. This book provides a fascinating look at personality types and temperaments. You'll discover how your temperament affects your success in relationships, careers, and life in general.

Tobias, Cynthia Ulrich. *Every Child Can Succeed: Making the Most of Your Child's Learning Style.* Colorado Springs: Focus on the Family, 1995. This book is filled with practical ideas for applying learning styles to motivation, discipline, and much more. Copyright-free profiles contained in the appendix can help parents and children record and summarize learning-style strengths for their teachers.

Tobias, Cynthia Ulrich. *I Hate School: How to Help Your Child Love Learning.* Grand Rapids, MI: Zondervan, 2004. This book offers dozens of practical strategies for helping education fit the child instead of insisting that a precious and uniquely designed child must always simply adjust to the methods provided.

Tobias, Cynthia Ulrich. *The Way They Learn: How to Discover and Teach to Your Child's Strengths.* Colorado Springs: Focus on the Family, 1994. An international bestseller, this entertaining and practical book should be required reading for any parent or teacher who truly wants to help his children succeed. These concepts are powerful tools for bringing out the best in every child.

Tobias, Cynthia Ulrich. *The Way We Work: A Practical Approach for Dealing with People on the Job.* Nashville: Broadman & Holman, 1999. An enlightening and easy-to-read resource for developing more efficient communication with those with whom you work. This is a powerful plan for transforming your on-the-job relationships!

Cynthia Ulrich Tobias, M.Ed.

Author of Focus on the Family's best-selling book *The Way They Learn*, Cynthia Tobias has a successful background that includes more than twenty-five years of private practice, eight years of teaching high school, and six years in law enforcement. She has authored eight books, is a featured guest on radio and television, and is a popular presenter for businesses, government agencies, churches, and schools throughout the United States and around the world.